AF334885

CONTENTS

Use Guide

PART ONE

COVENANT--THE BIBLICAL STORY

Wolfgang Roth

1

COVENANT-A FIRST ORIENTATION

Where do we begin the biblical story of the covenant? We could begin with the first book of the Old Testament, the Book of Genesis, because it speaks of God's covenants with Noah (Genesis 9) and with Abraham (Genesis 17). But the study of the Old Testament in the last one hundred years has shown us that in these chapters we encounter a fully developed and relatively late notion of the covenant. It is important and will be fully discussed, yet this is not where the story of the covenant properly *begins.*

Where then does our story begin? It starts as a full-fledged story a century or so earlier—more exactly, shortly before the Babylonian Exile. At that time (621 B.C.) a reformation took place in ancient Israel comparable to the reform movements in church history. That reformation was carried out by King Josiah (see 2 Kings 22-23); its spirit and course were determined to a large extent by the Book of Deuteronomy. Here the notion of covenant is important, even central.

Thus we begin our story with those texts and the events they describe. This has the added advantage that we lay hold of the biblical covenant notion where it is consciously stressed and put into the center. Here we meet sacred writers who set out, like we do now, to claim God's presence with his people anew. They did this by using the concept of the covenant—a concept known to them both from political covenants into which nations entered with each other and also from sacred tradition where secular and religious covenants had appeared from time to time.

Our story continues. We briefly explore other ways in which the people of the Old Testament speak of God's presence among them. In all cases we are made aware that ancient Israel saw itself as an elected people. Israelites understood themselves as set apart for a purpose: the service of God and humankind. Yet nowhere was Israel's election sealed and affirmed in a clearer fashion than in its covenant with the Lord God of Israel.

This leads us to look more broadly at covenant passages scattered throughout the Hebrew Scriptures. We formulate a working definition according to which "covenant" is not so much a legal contract which settles and limits claims the contractors may have toward each other. Rather,

---

a covenant relates the partners as whole persons (or communities) to each other and makes them (fictitious) sisters or brothers of each other. It is a flexible relationship where trust and faithfulness to each other determine the action of the partners.

When God is a covenant partner, he remains the Lord yet binds himself to his people. Various biblical passages can be interpreted and seen together in the light of this definition, adding details and additional aspects to the emerging story of the covenant. We note recent studies which show that in the ancient world political covenants were initiated, set up, and concluded according to certain patterns—and that these patterns influenced biblical notions of the covenant. The merits of the covenant concept then claim our attention and bring us to the aspects which were debated in biblical times.

The four aspects of the covenant which were debated can be summarized by these questions: (1) How exclusive is the covenant relationship? (2) How universal and comprehensive is it? (3) Can the covenant be primarily related to the inner life of the partners, forgoing external rites of initiation or observance? (4) How enduring is the covenant relationship? Can it be annulled or superseded by a new covenant?

Then our story tells how, in the first centuries of our era, synagogue and church picked up the idea of the covenant. For the Jews the covenant granted long ago to Israel still stands; it is everlasting. Once for all it makes known God's presence with his people and God's will for his people. But for many Christians the death of Jesus is the seal of a new covenant; it sets them apart from the synagogue and turns the covenant from Mount Sinai into the *old* covenant. Thus the covenant theme becomes enshrined in the sacred writings of synagogue and church in a twofold manner: for the Jews it is an eternal covenant, valid once for all; for the Christians a new covenant has been granted through Jesus Christ. Yet both communions treasure the covenant motif and sometimes use it in parallel ways. It binds the two communities to each other more than it separates them!

The covenant theme comes to life again in the time of the Reformation and in North America. The second part of this book traces the impact of the motif in these periods. It brings the story of the covenant to our time and place and invites us to reclaim it—well aware of the inner tensions and the outer edges, of the constructive possibilities and the dehumanizing abuses of the covenant. So our covenant story closes the circle: we are once again addressed as the people of the covenant and invited into a bond that sets us free for each other. We are once again what covenant-participants before us were: persons taken seriously as humans beings, living as partners with each other.

2.

ISRAEL - THE COVENANTED PEOPLE

a. Deuteronomy and Covenant

The time was ripe. The little kingdom of Judah under King Josiah found itself almost free from the shadow of the Assyrian empire. The rule of the cruel overlords from the land of the Tigris was coming to an end; in the year 612 B.C. their capital Nineveh fell to the Babylonians. For the people and the king of Judah the change of political fortune promised freedom, a new lease on life. Energetic and farsighted King Josiah read the signs of the times. He wanted to restore the empire of his forebear, King David. More than three hundred years before, it had spanned all of Palestine and commanded respect and tribute from those who had been made part of King David's realm. The golden age of David and of his son Solomon inspired this young king of the late seventh century B.C. to build an empire centered in Jerusalem, a kingdom like David's.

In the course of the restoration King Josiah also turns to the restoration of the temple in Jerusalem, the royal sanctuary. Here stands the Ark of the Covenant which David had set up to make his new political capital (Jerusalem) also the religious center of the Israelites. We read in 2 Kings 22 that in the course of the restoration of the temple, the officiating priest finds a book. He reads that book and is struck by what it proclaims. He promptly brings it to the king and the king has it read in the presence of the court. Then the ruler enquires of a prophetess about the strange find. She confirms that it is indeed a message from the God of Israel. So the king proceeds to implement the words of "the book of the covenant which had been found."

The king then moves to purge the religion as practiced in the land and at the temple. We also hear of his further action in 2 Kings 23:1-3:

> Then the king sent, and all the elders of Judah and Jerusalem were gathered to him. And the king went up to the house of the Lord, and with him all the men of Judah and all the inhabitants of Jerusalem, and the priests and the prophets, all the people, both small and great; and he read in their hearing all the words of the book of the covenant which had been found in the house of the Lord. And the king stood by the pillar and made a covenant before the Lord, to walk after the Lord and to keep his commandments and his testimonies and his statutes, with all his heart and all his soul, to perform the words of this covenant that were written in this book; and all the people joined in the covenant.

The language, the pattern, and the concept of the covenant between the Lord and his people is found time and again in the Old Testament. It is one of the important elements in the religion of ancient Israel. Josiah's covenant is made before the Lord, putting upon the people the obligation to observe the Lord's commandments and to obey his will as laid down in his commandments. The people are to do so wholeheartedly and in single-minded loyalty, "with all one's heart and all one's life." It is a covenant that binds both king and people, a covenant inclusive of the men of Judah and the inhabitants of Jerusalem. All layers of society are included—old and young, small and great, rich and poor, as well as the priests and the prophets.

Before we probe further into the nature of the covenant initiated by the startling find of "the book of the covenant" in the Temple, we note the suggestion of students of the Bible (among them some of the Church Fathers), that the book found in the temple is simply the core of the Book of Deuteronomy; more exactly, Deuteronomy 5-30. The argument in support of this thesis is a simple one: several of the measures of reform carried out by King Josiah are prescribed in the Book of Deuteronomy and *only* there. For instance, we hear of the centralization of all worship in Jerusalem and its temple, and of a purge of cults and priests elsewhere in the land. Furthermore, the thrust of Deuteronomy 5-30, its main emphases and themes, are identical with the spirit of the reform and restoration movement of King Josiah. Deuteronomy 5-30 shows us the forces at work in what is told in 2 Kings 22-23. Specifically, Deuteronomy 29:10-13 almost reads like the address King Josiah may have given when he concluded the covenant:

> You stand this day all of you before the Lord your God; the heads of your tribes, your elders, and your officers, all the men of Israel, your

> little ones, your wives, and the sojourner who is in your camp, both he who hews your wood and he who draws your water, that you may enter into the sworn covenant of the Lord your God, which the Lord your God makes with you this day; that he may establish you this day as his people, and that he may be your God, as he promised you, and as he swore to your fathers, to Abraham, to Isaac, and to Jacob. . . .

The goal of the covenant relationship is crucial: a mutuality between the Lord, the God of Israel, and his people Israel.

In this mutuality comes to fruition what had been promised already to Israel's fathers long before Moses. It spans the centuries and does not come to an end in the present! The Deuteronomic preacher-king may have continued (29:14-15):

> Nor is it with you only that I make this sworn covenant, but with him who is not here with us this day as well as with him who stands here with us this day before the Lord our God.

What are the basic themes of this covenant concluded in the time of Josiah before the Lord, and including the whole people of Israel? We turn to Deuteronomy 7: 6-11 for one of the clearest answers to our question:

> For you are a people holy to the Lord your God; the Lord your God has chosen you to be a people for his own possession, out of all the peoples that are on the face of the earth. It was not because you were more in number than any other people that the Lord set his love upon you and chose you, for you were the fewest of all peoples; but it is because the Lord loves you, and is keeping the oath which he swore to your fathers, that the Lord has brought you out with a mighty hand, and redeemed you from the house of bondage, from the hand of Pharaoh king of Egypt. Know therefore that the Lord your God is God, the faithful God who keeps covenant and steadfast love with those who love him and keep his commandments, to a thousand generations, and requites to their face those who hate him, by destroying them; . . . . You shall therefore be careful to do the commandment, and the statutes, and the ordinances, which I command you this day.

The key themes of the covenant of Deuteronomy are here set forth. We note the exclusivity of the relation between Israel and its God. They are singled out to be his people and his people only. (This is the meaning of the term "to be holy to the Lord".) This exclusiveness demands single-minded loyalty of both partners to each other. It is a relationship that excludes other loyalties. In fact, those who turn away from the covenantal partner–from their God–find themselves threatened with destruction.

The mutual loyalty is based on God's love for Israel and makes the relationship between the Lord and his people a relationship of love. It is covenantal love. It originates with the Lord God of Israel; he is the one who loved Israel first. It is a love based not on any merit of the Israelites nor on their great numbers. In response to this love of the Lord, Israel responds to him in single-minded loyalty in a way which is classically put in the text cherished by Jews and Christians alike:

> Hear, O Israel: The Lord our God is one Lord; and you shall love the Lord your God with all your heart, and with all your soul, and with all your might. (Deut. 6:4-5)

Jesus first answered the question about which is the greatest commandment by quoting this passage. It confesses God the Lord as the one God to whom human beings are invited to turn in unbounded love. Jesus then quoted Leviticus 19:18, which enjoins love to one's neighbor (Mark 12:28-34, cf. Matthew 22:34-40; Luke 10:25-28).

The love of the Lord for Israel is the key to both past and future. The Lord chose Israel and entered into a covenantal relationship with them because he loved them. He will stay in that covenantal relationship with them because he has turned to them in love. This love makes him both their protector and the one who supplies them with the good things of life here and now. This love set Israel free from bondage in Egypt so as to give them the land of promise with all its blessings, "a land flowing with milk and honey."

The covenantal relationship envisioned in the Book of Deuteronomy, as it stands behind Josiah's covenant in 2 Kings 23, is characterized by this exclusive, single-minded, mutual loyalty. The covenant's emphasis is on the one Lord, Israel's God. He has chosen this one people Israel to live before him in gratefulness on the one land he gave them as token of his love. They are to worship at the one holy place where he has chosen "to put his name" (Deuteronomy 12:5). They are to be guided by the one prophetic voice which the Lord raises among them as a successor to Moses, the supreme prophet of old. Israel's king is to be a part of this covenant; he is in no way singled out. He remains one of the Israelites, a brother sharing with them the gifts Israel's God has bestowed on them.

How does God order his relationship to his people? How do God's people order their relationship to him? *By covenant only* is the Deuteronomic response. The notion of covenant is central to this book of the Old Testament. It is also crucial in the historical books Joshua, Judges, 1 and 2 Samuel, 1 and 2 Kings, which in their outlook are closely related to Deuteronomy. Here, in these old narratives, we have a comprehensive review of the history of ancient Israel from the entry into the land of promise to the exile from that land.

These historical books conceive Israel's history as God's covenanting with his people—a covenant in which time and again Israel broke away from its divine covenant partner, a history in which time and again that divine covenant partner sought to restore the covenantal relationship. In the time of Josiah and not long before the disaster of the Babylonian Exile, when the political situation called for political restoration and religious reformation, Deuteronomy was that centering of Israel's traditions which made Josiah's short-lived political success possible. Moreover, the idea of the covenant emerged in the Israel at the verge of destruction as the key pattern, the key theme, suited to comprehend Israel's past, present, and even its future. It was classically formulated in the covenant formula according to which the Lord was to be their God and they were to be his people.

It is significant that the Hebrew word which to a large extent corresponds to the English word "covenant" occurs almost 100 times in the books of Deuteronomy, Joshua, Judges, Samuel and Kings. A third of all its occurrences in the Old Testament are found in these books. In other words, *covenant* is one of the key themes of the historical books and the Book of Deuteronomy.

The concept of the covenant and the single-minded loyalty of the covenantal partners to each other was to shape history, thought and Scriptures of ancient Israel in the centuries that followed. Its simplicity, its straightforwardness, its inclusiveness, and the zeal with which it was set forth—all these qualities made an impact on the prophets of the exile, on historians who speak to us from the early post-exilic period, on early Judaism, and also on the early Church. In fact, "covenant" was translated into Latin and became for the Christians the word by which their sacred Scriptures were named. *Testamentum* becomes the Christian name for the Hebrew Scriptures as Old Testament and the Christian Scriptures as New Testament.

b. Election and Covenant

The Old Testament uses various words and concepts in order to refer to God's choice of Israel. The Hebrew verb "to choose" is often used, as in the classical passage Deuteronomy 7:6-8. It refers to a free, unmotivated selection of one from among many possible choices. Thus the election of Israel is a choice made by God, selecting Israel from among the many nations who live on earth. Other words used with reference to God's election throw light on other aspects of God's act. Prophets refer to Israel's election as God's call of Israel, thereby indicating God's sovereign command and action (Hosea 11:1). It can also be said that God has acquired or purchased his people, thereby referring to God's intention of making Israel his own (Exodus 15:16, Psalm 74:2). Priestly writers stress that God has set Israel apart for holiness: "You shall be holy to me; for I the Lord am holy, and have separated you from the peoples, that you should be mine" (Leviticus 20:26).

A variety of figurative expressions of election are found in the Old Testament. The relationship can be compared to that between a father and son, emphasizing the intimacy of the relationship and the confidence that prevails in Israel's dependence upon God (Hosea 11:1, Deuteronomy 8:5, cf. Romans 8:14). Israel's sonship was not thought of as a physical or metaphysical one but was described by way of comparison. Elsewhere we find the picture of the marriage union, stressing the love and care of the Lord for his people. This comparison was first used by Hosea, a prophet of the Northern Kingdom, and then became part of the biblical tradition and was used there in various ways (Hosea 2:19-20, Jeremiah 2:2-3, Ezekiel 16:8, cf. Ephesians 5:31-32).

Sometimes the relationship is compared with a shepherd and his flock, emphasizing the considerate care and guidance which God affords his people (Psalms 68:7-10, 23:1-4, cf. John 10:11, Hebrews 13:20, 1 Peter 2:25). More impersonal but equally forceful is the comparison with the husbandman in his relation to his vineyard (Isaiah 5:1-7, Jeremiah 12:10, cf. Matthew 20:1-15). Jeremiah's vision shows God as the potter in whose hands Israel is like clay (Jeremiah 18:6). Finally, Israel can be described as God's own possession, a kingdom of priests and a holy nation (Exodus 19:5-6).

These passages make clear that Israel as a people, corporately, was and is elected by its Lord. This election-consciousness was born in Israel when, against all expectations, God the Lord set a weak, dispirited, helpless people free from slavery in Egypt and delivered them miraculously from their pursuers. In this deliverance God's choice became evident to the eyes of faith. The history of Israel bears witness to Israel's belief that God set them apart through an act of his will. This faith underlies many traditions alive in ancient Israel–traditions which were later committed to writing and found their place in the Old Testament.

The protests of the prophets show that Israel was constantly in danger of forgetting the purpose of its election. Israel's special position was not an end in itself nor did it find its fulfillment in itself. It was election for a purpose! Not as some apocalyptic seers later saw it as a fulfillment in a future and other-worldly realm, Israel's purpose was to be God's presence in this world here and now in a wide, comprehensive sense. It was service both *of* God and *for* God (compare Mark 12:28-31). Service of God insofar as Israel worships the Lord and him alone: "... now, Israel, what does the Lord your God require of you, but to fear the Lord your God, to walk in all his ways, to love him, to serve the Lord your God with all your heart and with all your soul ..." (Deuteronomy 10:12).

In this way the people of the Lord fulfill here and now the commission given to them when they entered the covenant: to be a kingdom of priests and a holy nation.

The purpose of election is also service *on behalf of* God. As such, it is directed to all of God's creation and is universal in scope. This is already clear in the call of the father of Israel, Abraham, who is to be a blessing for "all the families of the earth" (Genesis 12:3).

The emphasis on Israel's universal mission is not found equally in all parts of the Old Testament. The Deuteronomic and the priestly writers tended to preach holiness and stress separation from all that could possibly pollute Israel's faith and worship, especially Canaanite practices (Deuteronomy 4:19, Leviticus 18:2-3). On the other hand, some of the prophets emphasized Israel's universal obligation; an example is the prophecy found both in Isaiah 2:2-4 and Micah 4:1-4. In the future "all the nations shall flow to" Mount Zion in order to be taught God's ways and walk in his paths.

Isaiah of Babylon, an anonymous prophet whose words are found in the Book of Isaiah, chapters 40-55 (also known as Second Isaiah), was the one who forcefully reminded Israel of its universal obligation. In the judgment of many scholars, he manifests a universal outlook when he invites "all the ends of the earth" to turn to the Lord and thus to be saved (Isaiah 45:22). The worldwide scope of Israel's election is fully realized by the anonymous figure of the Suffering Servant who represents the fullness of the prophetic office in Israel. To him God says: "It is too light a thing that you should be my servant to raise up the tribes of Jacob and to restore the preserved of Israel; I will give you as a light to the nations, that my salvation may reach to the ends of the earth" (Isaiah 49:6, cf. 42:6).

This note is echoed in the words of the prophet Malachi when he affirms that "from the rising of the sun to its setting my name is great among the nations" (Malachi 1:11) and in the exhortation of the Psalmist: "Praise the Lord, all nations! Extol him, all peoples!" (Psalm 117:1).

Israel was conscious of its election from the earliest times. The election relationship called for ways in which it could be made visible and tangible, as shown by the variety of images discussed in this section. However, the concept of the covenant of God with Israel is frequently used to make this election manifest; the covenant is the seal of election.

We now turn to the next question: What is "covenant" in the Bible? In what ways is it described? How is it understood more broadly?

3.

COVENANT IN THE HEBREW SCRIPTURES

The pattern of covenant was so central in the Hebrew Scriptures that it made a strong impact. Thus, Jesus at the last supper says to his disciples when they have drunk from the cup: "This is my blood of the (new) covenant, which is poured out for many" (Mark 14:24). Some ancient manuscripts of the Greek text of the New Testament here add the word "new" before the word "covenant," contrasting what is initiated through Jesus with what was done by Moses. The idea of covenant also occurs in the Letter to the Hebrews where we read that Jesus is "the mediator of a new covenant" (9:15).

In the course of the Church's history we encounter the concept of covenant—for instance, in John Wesley's covenant service. This is observed on New Year's Eve and designed to bring the year-to-come under the sovereignty of God. In our time, church manuals sometimes refer to the marriage union as a covenant made between a man and a woman. In fact, marriage is an example of what a covenant is. It is not only a legal agreement between partners, even though such an agreement is one aspect of it. It is not merely a ceremony of importance, even though a solemn initiation belongs to a covenant. It is not a vaguely defined relationship which can be ignored in unfavorable circumstances or canceled at will. A covenant is a communion between partners, solemnly initiated, binding the partners into a new pattern of life, and letting them mutually define each other. It affects all aspects of the partners' lives, creating between and for them a sphere of interaction in loyalty to each other.

Word and notion of covenant are not current today. In the ancient Orient, in ancient Israel, and in civilizations related to the biblical heritage, covenant or covenant-like relationships were the form into which social and religious communal life was shaped. Indeed, some aspects of North American life have been shaped directly and indirectly by biblical covenant patterns and traditions. (See the second part of this book.) A covenant is a more comprehensive and less legally defined relationship than a contract. A contract relates only to specific aspects or claims of human relationships; it seeks to regulate them according to a fixed standard. The covenant relates to persons as whole human beings; it humanizes interpersonal relationships.

In the Old Testament itself and in ancient Near Eastern texts we read of different kinds of covenants. They were concluded between partners who had stood in an uncertain, strained, or even hostile relationship with each other–partners who wished to end such threatening relations and establish secure, clearly defined patterns of life. Making a covenant is like creating a (fictitious) blood relationship between the partners who then become brothers or sisters. This can be seen in Laban's covenant with Jacob where the uneasy peace which prevails between them is turned into a secure and clearly defined relationship through the conclusion of a covenant (Genesis 31:25-54, esp. 44-54). Another example is the deception of Joshua by the Gibeonites who manage to trick the Israelite leader into concluding a covenant with them. They thus escape destruction and win a secure, albeit subordinate position within Israel (Joshua 9). We also see the covenant which David, the man aspiring to be king, concludes with Jonathan, the son of King Saul, who was a possible contender for the throne of his father. The deep friendship between the two is not considered secure in these circumstances until it has been sealed through a covenant (1 Samuel 18:1-3).

Covenants were solemnly initiated. We hear of oaths sworn, meals eaten together, witnesses called upon, the exchange of clothes worn by partners, and covenant stipulations–that is, of directions for the future course of action and binding the partners (Genesis 31:46-49, 53, 54; 1 Samuel 18:4, Genesis 31:50, Joshua 9:18-19).

In a few cases the covenant was initiated by a solemn rite. Animals were cut in half and the pieces laid out on the ground, one opposite the other. Then the covenant partners walked together between the bloody pieces (cf. Genesis 15:7-21, Jeremiah 34:18). This peculiar ritual is also known from non-biblical ancient Near Eastern texts. It was a solemn affirmation that in case one of the covenant partners did not abide in the covenant, then God, who was universally considered the protector of covenants, would make the unfaithful partner "like the calf which they cut in two and passed between its parts" (Jeremiah 34:18). A threat like this illustrates the seriousness of the covenant relationship.

Once established, the covenant brought about unity of the partners. Between them existed harmony and wholeness. To characterize this concord, the Old Testament frequently employed words derived from a root *sh-l-m.* It refers in its various forms to completeness, to perfection, to peace, prosperity and well-being. It is the word *shalom* (Genesis 26:31, Isaiah 54:10, Jeremiah 33:9, Numbers 25:12, Psalms 119:165, and 125:5).

The Deuteronomic preachers and historians who penned Deuteronomy and the historical books Joshua, Judges, Samuel and Kings, also employ this word. They use *shalom* to describe the covenant partner as "wholly true" to the other partner. For instance, when Solomon ends the dedication prayer of his newly built temple, he admonishes the people: "Let your heart therefore be wholly true *(sh-l-m)* to the Lord our God, walking in his statutes and keeping his commandments . . . " (1 Kings 8: 61).

On the other hand, the aging Solomon is chastised by the historians for letting himself be seduced by his foreign wives into worshipping foreign gods. In 1 Kings 11:4 we read that when Solomon became old, his wives "turned away his heart" so that he worshipped other gods. Then his life was no more "wholly true" *(sh-l-m)* to the Lord his God, in contrast to David his father. Also other kings were judged positively or negatively by the historian, depending on how fully they lived in covenantal loyalty with God and fellow human beings (1 Kings 15:3; 2 Kings 23:25). Thus the covenant is the opposite of insecurity, enmity, and uncontrolled behavior. There is no stronger guarantee of security, of personal faithfulness and of peace between the covenant partners than the formal establishment of a covenantal relationship.

Israel believed that God had entered into a covenant with them. Prepared by the promises of God to the patriarchs, the covenant was granted to Israel at Mount Sinai through Moses, the covenant mediator. The oldest tradition concerning this covenant comes from wise men who compiled the story of Israel's beginnings and who speak to us in many texts in the Pentateuch. The passage Exodus 24:9-11 is part of their contribution. It tells of a meal which the elders of Israel, under the leadership of Moses, held on the sacred mountain. This meal was part of the covenant initiation ceremony. In other texts in the Pentateuch the story of God granting the covenant appears in different forms. For instance, we have a more prophetically-oriented version in Exodus 24:3-8, one from a priestly view in Exodus 31:16, and one from the mouth of the Deuteronomic preachers in Deuteronomy 5:2.

While the old story of the covenant initiation told by wise men (Exodus 24:1-2, 9-11) stresses Moses as the sole mediator of the covenant, the more prophetically-oriented version (Exodus 24:3-8) stresses the people's participation. (Their share is symbolized by twelve pillars, one for each of the twelve tribes of Israel.) The priestly version emphasizes the observance of the sabbath:

". . . the people of Israel shall keep the sabbath, observing the sabbath throughout their generations, as a perpetual covenant" (Exodus 31:16). And the Deuteronomic preachers stress that the covenant once made cannot be relegated to the past: "The Lord our God made a covenant with us in Horeb. Not with our fathers did the Lord make this covenant, but with us, who are all of us here alive this day" (Deuteronomy 5:2-3).

The covenant theme is echoed in the words of the prophets, but they view Israel's actions as betrayal of the covenant. Hosea calls out in the name of his God: "Set the trumpet to your lips, for a vulture is over the house of the Lord, because they have broken my covenant, and transgressed my law" (8:1). Jeremiah prays on behalf of his people and implores God not to give them up to their enemies. He pleads with the Lord not to dishonor his glorious throne (the city and temple of Jerusalem); he calls on God to remember and not to break his covenant with them (14:21).

Ezekiel pleads with his listeners in the name of God and reminds them of their entrance into a covenant with God:

> When I passed by you . . . you were at the age for love; and I spread my skirt over you, and covered your nakedness: yea, I plighted my troth to you and entered into a covenant with you, says the Lord God, and you became mine. (Ezek. 16:8)

Note how the covenant is seen here as a marriage relationship. Moreover, the prophet uses it boldly even though among the Canaanites such language was used with reference to the deity as the one who impregnates the soil.

Certainly one of the most moving references to God's covenant with Israel is found in the words of comfort spoken by an unknown prophet, commonly known as Second Isaiah, in the name of his God. The words are directed to Israel in exile, driven away from the land of promise and sinking into despair, as of old all creation drowned in the waters of The Great Flood:

> For this is like the days of Noah to me: as I swore that the waters of Noah should no more go over the earth, so I have sworn that I will not be angry with you and will not rebuke you. For the mountains may depart and the hills be removed, but my steadfast love shall not depart from you, and my covenant of peace shall not be removed, says the Lord, who has compassion on you. (Isa. 54:9-10)

The psalmists also sing of God's covenant. In a lament which describes all the sufferings an individual may have to endure, the assurance is voiced: "The friendship of the Lord is for those who fear him, and he makes known to them his covenant" (Psalm 25:14).

Another psalmist assures in his song of thanksgiving that God "is mindful of his covenant for ever, of the word that he commanded, for a thousand generations" (Psalm 105:8).

Even in the visions of apocalyptic seers the covenant theme is important. One of them, speaking to us in Zechariah 9-14, assures his listeners that God will set Israel's captives free. This hope is founded, the prophet says, on God's covenant with the people, sealed through the application of blood (Zechariah 9:11; compare Exodus 24:3-8). In the Book of Daniel we find another apocalyptic voice reciting prayers and confessions. One of them begins: "O Lord, the great and terrible God, who keepest covenant and steadfast love with those who love him and keep his commandments . . . " (9:4).

Thus there can be no doubt that ancient Israel thought of God's relationship to this people as a covenant. To be sure, this was not stressed at all times and in all places in the history of ancient Israel in the same way. At times there was debate and tension in relation to the covenant and what it entailed for Israel and for non-Israelites. Yet for many writers of the Old Testament, covenant was the *form* which Israel's election took. Through the covenant God's election of Israel was sealed. God had bound himself clearly and visibly to this people. We may even define the relationship between election and covenant as that between word and sacrament, as commonly understood by Christians. The divine word given to this people was a word of promise, forgiveness and healing; it was sealed in the granting of covenants, much as in Christian understanding the sacraments seal God's presence among the people. The covenant with which the Lord bound himself to Israel is his election of Israel made visible.

Recent studies have shown that the covenant from Mount Sinai and its later reflections in the Old Testament, especially as unfolded in Deuteronomy and Josiah's reform (2 Kings 22-23), have parallels in ancient Near Eastern political treaties, particulary those concluded by Hittite emperors with their vassals in the second millennium before Christ. These were solemn agreements made at the instance of the ruler of the Hittite empire with defeated or weaker kings. They were bound by a covenant to stay in allegiance and act in loyalty to their overlord. He in turn afforded his vassals security, protection, and help, safeguarding peace and prosperity within the whole realm.

Detailed studies have shown a covenantal pattern to be at work in covenant texts. A sequence of six elements is usually found in these vassal treaties. A comparison with the description of the covenant from Mount Sinai, especially as found in the Book of Deuteronomy, suggests that ancient Israel used this ancient Oriental pattern in order to understand itself as the people of the Lord–as the vassals of God on the earth. Deuteronomy sets it forth very well: God is Israel's divine overlord who has graciously granted the security and peace which result from a vassal covenant. To him Israel owes exclusive allegiance and service. Hence God the Lord is sometimes spoken of as the supreme king whose place nobody must usurp. This is well illustrated in Gideon's words when he has been invited to become Israel's king after defeating the Midianites. Gideon rejects that demand, saying: "I will not rule over you, and my son will not rule over you; the Lord will rule over you" (Judges 8:23).

Similarly, Exodus 15:18 ends the song of Israel's deliverance from Egyptian oppression with the words: "The Lord will reign for ever and ever." And Psalm 29:10 praises God who "sits enthroned as king for ever."

On the other hand, Israel knows itself set into a sphere of peace and well-being which made life worth living. The references to God's covenant of peace show this most clearly. (See Isaiah 54:10). The offer of the covenant is thus the offer of life itself:

> See, I have set before you this day life and good, death and evil . . . I call heaven and earth to witness against you this day, that I have set before you life and death, blessing and curse; therefore choose life. . . . (Deut. 30:15-19)

To conclude our discussion of the covenant as the form which God's election took, it is important to point out the advantages of the covenant concept. We here follow the discussion of the topic by the Old Testament scholar Walter Eichrodt in his *Theology of the Old Testament* (English translation, published by Westminster Press).

First, by its very nature the covenant reminds all who stand within it that covenants have always been initiated by God's action. It is always

God who maintains the covenant. Israel's faith—its very existence—are based on God's prior action in history. The covenant is a constant reminder of this.

Second, through the covenant stipulations God's will is clearly known. There is no room for the fear of an unknown God whose will is inscrutable and into whose hand man is mercilessly surrendered. Through the covenant, an atmosphere of confidence and security is created. Israel has been given room for a full and right life within the covenant relationship.

Third, the granting of the covenant unites those who accept its obligations into the one people of God. The Israelite tribes and families belong together not primarily on account of their blood and kinship, but because together they acknowledge one divine overlord. In a sense, the concept of the kingdom of God was born here. Allegiance and loyalty to the Lord as the supreme king defined the limits of his kingdom. The covenant is the basis of the corporate life of the people of God.

Fourth, the covenant relationship does justice to God's freedom. He as divine overlord is not irrevocably bound to the people of his choice, especially when Israel does not conform to the stipulations. God can reject Israel and the prophets affirm that he will certainly do so if they do not return to the Lord and thus live (Amos 5:4-14). There even arises, in the despair of the Babylonian exile, the hope that God's history with Israel has not come to an end but that he will conclude a new covenant to replace the first, which Israel has broken (Jeremiah 31:31-34, Ezekiel 36: 22-23; compare Isaiah 43:18-21).

On the other hand, there can be no doubt that Israel misunderstood the character of the covenant by forgetting God's freedom and by treating the covenant as what we may call a legal arrangement. The legalism that prevailed in some circles of later Judaism, as well as in certain Christian circles, is such a misunderstanding. When our Lord condemned this legalism, he protested against thinking of Israel's relationship with God in terms of legal contract or even as a bargain. Thus Jesus, according to the Evangelist Luke, does not see the human being's relationship to God as one governed by the desire for reward:

> So you also, when you have done all that is commanded you, say, "We are unworthy servants; we have only done what was our duty." (Luke 17:10)

Similarly, a Jewish teacher of the first centuries of the Christian era warns against a legalistic misunderstanding of the divine-human relationship:

> Do not be like servants who serve the master for the sake of receiving a reward; rather be like servants who serve the master not for the sake of receiving a reward. (Pirke Aboth 1:3)

Finally, the covenant relationship makes clear and final the revelation of the name of God and the announcement of God's will and purpose. Its word becomes the medium of revelation: "God spoke . . . " (Exodus 20:1, and often in the Old Testament). Israel is related to its God through the word which he speaks in his freedom, and which accomplishes that for which it is sent. One may summarize this aspect of the covenant (as did Gerhard von Rad) in a way that foreshadows what was to occur in Jesus in the eyes of the early Christian movement:

---

while in the Old Testament the word of God became action, in the New Testament the word of God became flesh.

4.

THE EDGES OF COVENANT

a. How Inclusive?

The Deuteronomic preachers set forth an impressive covenant theology. It was imposing in its simplicity, in its straightforwardness, in its appeal. It was also an unbroken understanding because the Israel of King Josiah's period enjoyed days of security and peace. Yet all this was of short duration. Very soon the Babylonian Empire under its King Nebuchadnezzar was to cast its shadow again across the lands of the ancient Near East. The able Babylonian emperor conquered Syria and Palestine and appeared at the gates of Jerusalem. Twice Jerusalem was taken by him (597 and 587 B.C.). The first time it was not razed, but its king was sent into exile together with the elite of the kingdom of Judah. Heavy tribute was imposed on the little kingdom. An uncle of the deposed king was put on the throne by the Babylonian emperor and renamed Zedekiah. He rebelled ten years later.

In 587 B.C. Nebuchadnezzar's armies again stood before Jerusalem—this time to wipe out the rebellious city and its kingdom. Jerusalem fell to the Babylonians, it was razed, and its leading citizens were either executed or exiled. (See 2 Kings 25.) The king himself had to witness his sons butchered before he was blinded and led away as a common prisoner. Again the land was denuded of its leading citizens. A humble remnant remained to till the land, and to forward the heavy tribute which the Babylonians imposed.

Those who had been exiled to Mesopotamia were allowed to live in colonies. They lived as foreigners in a strange land, depressed and in despair. Psalm 137:1-3 movingly illustrates this:

> By the waters of Babylon, there we sat down and wept, when we remembered Zion. On the willows there we hung up our lyres. For there our captors required of us songs, and our tormentors, mirth, saying, "Sing us one of the songs of Zion!"

It is difficult to imagine how radical a break the exile was for the Judeans. They were bereft of their king and of their royal house, of priests and cultic ministrations, of temple and palace. Most of all, they were bereft of the land, their inheritance—the land "flowing with milk and honey" promised to them of old, given to them many centuries earlier as token of their election—a gift of the God of Israel to his people.

How, under these new circumstances, would the faith of Israel and the traditions inherited from the fathers be kept alive? For many, the situation meant a radical break with the past. They let themselves be absorbed into the land, the culture, and the religion of exile; they merged with the people among whom they lived. For some it meant desperately holding on to the traditions, the practices, and the observances of the past. They ignored the new situation and continued to live in the past; they simply denied the catastrophe that had struck. For still others it meant doubt and questioning, uncertainty and the search for an answer. The letter of Jeremiah to the exiles (Jeremiah 29) is an instructive example of such questions and the prophetic direction given by Jeremiah. He exhorts the people neither to give up the legacy of their past nor to hold to it in such an exclusive, narrow-minded fashion that they would no longer be able to live in their new land. They are to build houses and to plant vineyards there; they are to give their daughters into marriage and take daughters for their sons because the well-being of their new land is their well-being! So the prophet Jeremiah saw the new situation.

Small wonder that such questioning led to new ways of understanding the sacred traditions of Israel. In fact, the agony of the exile surfaced tensions and possibilities dormant in Israel's legacy. Rites and ceremonies possible only when the Israelites lived in Palestine moved into the background. On the other hand, ceremonies which could be observed anywhere and anytime became important. Two examples were the circumcision of the male infant as a sign of his becoming part of the people holy to the Lord, and the hallowing of the Sabbath as a day of rest and soon also as a day of worship and praise.

The writings of the Old Testament from the late pre-exilic and the exilic period show that the inherited idea of Israel as the covenanted people also became a matter of debate and questioning. Certain tensions inherent in the covenantal understanding of Israel's life asserted themselves under the strain of the exile. One of these was the old question as to how inclusive or how exclusive the covenant with the God of Israel is. Did God make a covenant with all of Israel? With each individual member of the people? Or was the covenantal relationship focused in a special way in a person or persons set apart from the rest of the people? Was the king or the priest that special person with whom, primarily and first of all, the Lord God of Israel had made his covenant?

Of old there existed in ancient Israel, especially among the tribes of the central and northern highlands, the notion that God's covenant had indeed been made with *all* of Israel through Moses at Mount Sinai. There they *all* had been called to be a people set apart, a kingdom of priests and a holy nation. On their behalf the elders had concluded the covenant with God, eating and drinking before God on the holy mountain (Exodus 24: 3-8). This Mosaic covenant tradition was passed on among the Israelites settled in the central and northern highlands, those who later formed the kingdom of Israel with Samaria as its capital. Among these people, prophets such as Elijah and Hosea spoke. For them the covenant was inclusive. *Each* member of the people of Israel was included. Later it was even stressed that women and children, rich and poor are also included. Hence the comprehensive, inclusive understanding of the covenant in these circles. The prophet Amos in his own way attests to this when he addresses the whole family of the people of Israel with the words spoken in the name of his God ("You only have I known of all the families of the earth") implying that it is the whole people standing in the covenant relationship (Amos 3:2).

On the other hand, with the rise of King David and the establishment of his dynasty, the people in the southern kingdom of Judah believed in the unique election of David and his dynasty. He and the kings "from his loin," sitting on the throne in Jerusalem after him through more than 300 years of the existence of the kingdom of Judah, were thought to stand in a special covenant relationship with God. It was David who was elected! The people were only secondarily related to the Lord God of Israel, so to speak, through their king. We here encounter the Judean version of the ancient Near Eastern royal ideology. According to it, all the blessings of the divine sphere are mediated to the earth, to human beings and human society, through the office and person of the king. (See 2 Samuel 7 and Psalm 89.) Even though the word "covenant" is not used, it is evident that the Davidic royal house in Judah on the throne in Jerusalem is the primary covenant partner with the God of Israel.

David's empire split into two kingdoms after the death of David's son, Solomon. In the course of the next two centuries, the northern kingdom of Israel and the southern kingdom of Judah were sometimes at war with each other. Many times they were uneasy neighbors. The difference in the understanding of who the covenant partners were was crucial: in the north there was more emphasis on the whole people as God's covenant partners; in the south it was more on the king as God's partner.

In 722 B.C. the northern kingdom was swept off the map and its leading people were exiled. Samaria became an Assyrian province. Foreign people were brought in to settle in the region. To the south, though, the little kingdom of Judah remained in relative independence. Those northerners who cherished the Mosaic, inclusive covenant seem to have come to the kingdom of Judah as refugees. Two or three generations later they succeeded in contributing this inclusive perspective to a reform movement which climaxed in Josiah's reign, described in 2 Kings 22-23. In chapters 5-30 of the Book of Deuteronomy the spirit of this reform speaks to us. Here we find the inclusive understanding of the covenant God has made with all of Israel as his partners. *All* are embraced: rich and poor; small and great; men, women, and children; priests and prophets; kings and wise men. Indeed, even the foreigners and strangers are to participate as far as possible in the ceremonies of the covenanted people!

After all, Deuteronomy affirms, the Israelites know how the foreigner and the stranger feel, for they were foreigners and strangers long ago in Egypt. The king is not singled out in a special way as far as the relation with the divine is concerned. In fact, the most important demand made of the king is that he get for himself a copy of the book of God's law, withdraw to his chamber, and study it there (Deuteronomy 17: 18-20).

Even in the time of the prophet Isaiah, the king in Jerusalem could not claim for himself a position above reprimand. This is illustrated by the prophet Isaiah who spoke words of stern reproach to his royal lord (Isaiah 7:10-17). This is also shown by the words of the prophet Jeremiah to King Jehoiakim, who evidently exploited his people in order to build for himself beautiful palaces. The prophet said to that king:

> Do you think you are a king because you compete in cedar? Did not your father eat and drink and do justice and righteousness? Then it was well with him. He judged the cause of the poor and needy; . . . Is not this to know me? says the Lord. (Jer. 22:15-16)

In the new situation of the exile, the privileges of the king were gone. The Israelites found themselves either as exiles in a foreign land or as those who tilled their land to pay tribute to their new overlords.

Now we hear prophetic words which claim that the ancient promises made to David and to his house are translated to *all* of Israel. Thus Isaiah of Babylon "democratizes" the Davidic covenant. While of old that covenant had been related to the royal house, it is now to be applied to all the people. The prophet says in the name of his God:

> Incline your ear, and come to me; hear, that your soul may live; and I will make with you an everlasting covenant, my steadfast, sure love for David. Behold, I made him a witness to the peoples, a leader and commander for the peoples. Behold, you shall call nations that you know not, and nations that knew you not shall run to you, because of the Lord your God, and of the Holy One of Israel, for he has glorified you. (Isa. 55:3-5)

What once was David's privilege has now become the work and mission of all Israel, at least of those addressed by the prophet. What once was reserved for the highly placed person of the king is now common good and the mission of the whole people. The old ideal of the Mosaic covenant is regained here, in that the covenant includes *all* of Israel. No one is privileged by position of leadership; no hierarchic misunderstanding of the covenant is possible.

Yet in the early post-exilic period when those returned from exile had established themselves as a religious community centered in the rebuilt temple, the words of the Chronicler attest to an exclusive understanding of God's covenant with his people. (The Chronicler speaks to us in the historical work found in 1 and 2 Chronicles, Ezra and Nehemiah.) He claims that the covenant is granted only to the people in Jerusalem and Judah, to those descended from the inhabitants of the erstwhile kingdom of Judah. It is not a privilege extended to those who live to the north—that is, to the people who live in what was once the kingdom of Israel. They wish to share with the Judeans the rebuilding of the temple now that the exile is past. But they are not considered by the Judeans as of pure descent from ancient Israelite stock. Hence, they are no longer considered pure in their religion.

This exclusivist understanding of the covenant is strikingly illustrated by the words of a Judean king, addressed to the first king of the northern kingdom. The Chronicler has him say to the people in the north whom he considered apostates and no longer acceptable:

> Ought you not to know that the Lord God of Israel gave the kingship over Israel for ever to David and his sons by a covenant of salt? . . . And now you think to withstand the kingdom of the Lord in the hand of the sons of David, because you are a great multitude and have with you the golden calves which Jeroboam made you for gods. . . . But as for us,

> the Lord is our God, and we have not forsaken him. . . . For we keep the charge of the Lord our God, but you have forsaken him. Behold, God is with us at our head, and his priests with their battle trumpets to sound the call to battle against you. O sons of Israel, do not fight against the Lord, the God of your fathers; for you cannot succeed. (2 Chron. 13:5-12)

The Chronicler speaks for the early post-exilic congregation in highly exclusive terms. They and only they are the inheritors of the covenant of old. In fact, it is only David and his sons (by now no longer on the throne) who can legitimately claim to be the covenant partners of God. An exclusive understanding of the covenant relationship asserts itself here. It stands in stark contrast to the inclusive character of the covenant stressed by others in ancient Israel!

b. How Universal?

The times of upheaval and questioning which the exile brought to the Israelites surfaced yet another related tension of the inherited covenant. We noted how the Chronicler straightforwardly answered the question as to how exclusive the covenant is. It is very exclusive indeed! Only the sons of David and their legitimate descendants can claim God's covenant for themselves; those who do not stand within that line of continuity are excluded. This was the message of the Chronicler through the words of the Judean king facing his northern rival.

But it became not only a question of whether the covenant included all the Israelites, only some of them, or possibly even only those hierarchically privileged. Now the question also arose about how *universal* the covenant is. Was it made only with the Israelites? Where did this leave other peoples and nations with whom the Israelites had come into close contact, especially during the Babylonian exile? After all, now they had to live as a humble religious community in a corner of the Persian empire. Understandably, the question of continuity with the past exercised them greatly. Were they the legitimate descendants of the ancient Israelites? What about their identity as the people of God? For the Chronicler it was an exclusive faith: Israel alone was the legitimate heir of the ancient covenant.

However, some voices in the later writings of the Old Testament strongly protest this exclusivist understanding of the faith of ancient Israel and of its covenantal relationship with God. The little book of Jonah, which in its own right is really a parable, may stand as one example. As is the case with other parables found both in the Old Testament (for instance, Nathan's parable in 2 Samuel 12:1-4) and in the New Testament (for instance, the parables collected in Matthew 13), it would be a misunderstanding to ask what historical events and personages the story portrays. It would be a misunderstanding of the parable of the prodigal son to insist that it was a description of what actually happened. Similarly, the book of Jonah must be read as a parable which teaches the truth in pictures.

We do not know who composed the little book. Its language and thought indicate that it was penned in the post-exilic period, probably in the time of the Chronicler. But if the Chronicler wrote in order to defend and justify his exclusivist understanding of covenant and God's relation to Israel only, the writer of the parable of Jonah wrote in order to challenge and test such a position. The booklet is an attack on exclusivism. Creative tension surfaces when the particularity of Israel must be brought together with the universality of God's will.

The parable of Jonah was written in a time when priestly and Davidic circles in Jerusalem and Judea insisted on keeping pure and undefiled their "orthodox" faith. As legitimate as their concern was, pursued to the extreme it led to a hardening of religion into exclusivity. The prophet Jonah stands before us as a living symbol of this self-centered religion. He must learn the hard way that God is concerned not with Israel only! God's concern is as wide as his creation.

This profound insight appears in many writings of the Old Testament, including the compositions of the wise men who speak to us in some sections of the Book of Genesis. Abraham, the father of the faithful, is called from Mesopotamia to the Land of Canaan so that through his obedience and reception of God's blessing "all the families of the earth will bless themselves" (Genesis 12:3). Jonah's mission to Nineveh, eventually carried out by the prophet, is successful. "When God saw what they did, how they turned from their evil way, God repented of the evil which he had said he would do to them; and he did not do it" (Jonah 3:10). How much the parabler of Jonah is a disciple of the prophets becomes clear when we read the Book of Jonah as commentary on a passage such as Jeremiah 18:7-8. There we hear the prophet speaking in the name of his God:

> If at any time I declare concerning a nation or a kingdom, that I will pluck up and break down and destroy it, and if that nation, concerning which I have spoken, turns from its evil, I will repent of the evil that I intended to do to it.

The real reason why Jonah had refused to go to Nineveh is stated by him only at the end of the booklet:

> I pray thee, Lord, is this not what I said when I was yet in my country? That is why I made haste to flee to Tarshish; for I knew that thou art a gracious God and merciful, slow to anger, and abounding in steadfast love, and repentest of evil. (Jonah 4:2)

The words he used in the second half of the verse, referring to God's mercy, were the very words with which ancient Israel had praised God's goodness in worship and life through the centuries (Exodus 34:6-7, Deuteronomy 5:9-10, Psalm 145:8-9). At this point the parable becomes transparent. Jonah *does not wish* God to be gracious and merciful, slow to anger and of great kindness. In short, he repudiates the God of Abraham, Isaac, and Jacob—the God of the covenant.

Here is the core of the parable. The people of Israel, like Jonah, have through their narrow and exclusive attitude rejected the very faith they claim to profess. The parable is an appeal to the Israel of the post-exilic period. It is a prophetic invitation to recognize God's concern for the whole world and to become active bearers of that concern. At the end of the Book of Jonah could fittingly stand the question of St. Paul: "Or is God the God of Jews only? Is he not the God of Gentiles also?" (Romans 3:29).

What surfaces in the Chronicles, on the one hand, and in the Book of Jonah, on the other, is tension that had lain dormant in ancient Israel's understanding of covenant. Now it had become fully visible. How does God's covenant with Israel relate to the rest of God's world? Is it an exclusive covenant, only with Israel? Or does it have the universal scope which we find portrayed in the Book of Jonah? The struggle between exclusivism and particularism was to remain one of the tensions bequeathed to later generations both in church and synagogue. It was to worry discerning Jews and Christians more than once!

In the Old Testament itself we encounter an impressive response to this tension inherent in ancient Israel's covenant. It is found in priestly passages in the Books of Genesis and Exodus. We should note here that many students of the Old Testament assume that in the first five books of the Old Testament (the Pentateuch) we encounter four different and separable literary sources. Each recounts in its own way the story of Israel's beginnings. One strand speaks primarily from the perspective of the philosopher or the wise man. Another source speaks primarily from the viewpoint of the prophets. A third, the Deuteronomic strand, is strongly influenced by this prophetic perspective but has other elements in it. Finally, we have the story of Israel's beginning told from a cultic perspective. This priestly strand of the Pentateuch is strongly interested in questions of legitimacy and continuity, and portrays the institution of Israel's various cultic observances.

From these priestly circles has come down to us the most comprehensive understanding of God's covenant. Simply put, God's covenant is a manifold one. It was given in three successive stages. It embraces in the first instance *all* of God's creation; second, it separates from within God's creation *the descendants of Abraham only;* and third, from among the descendants of Abraham it singles out *Israel proper*—the descendants of Jacob, the first Israelite. To this threefold covenant correspond three stages of the revelation of the divine name. At first God is known only by the general ancient name for the deity (in English, "God"); by this name he is known to Noah and all humankind descended from Noah. In a second granting of a covenant, God makes himself known to Abraham and to his descendants by the special proper name "God Almighty." In the third, final, and most central grant of the covenant, God Almighty makes himself known by his own proper name, the Lord.

This is well set forth in the priestly passage Exodus 6:2-4. "God said to Moses, I am the Lord. I appeared to Abraham, to Isaac, and to Jacob, as God Almighty, but by my name the Lord I did not make myself known to them. I also established my covenant with them. . . . "

Three sacramental signs correspond to the threefold dispensation of the covenant. The rainbow is the covenantal sign given to Noah and to his descendants. "When the bow is in the clouds," says God to Noah, "I . . . remember the everlasting covenant between God and every living creature of all flesh . . ." (Genesis 9:16). No more shall the destruction which the Flood wrought come over the earth; from now on, God's will for all humankind is directed toward life and peace. For Hebrew readers and hearers the picture is made even more appealing because in Hebrew the word for "rainbow" is identical with the word for "warrior's bow." Hence when God sets his bow in the clouds, he puts it away as a weapon of war!

The sign connected with the second grant of the covenant is different. Upon Abraham and his descendants is laid the obligation of circumcision—that is, the removal of the foreskin of the penis. Through this rite each male child enters the covenant. Unlike the look at the rainbow, this covenantal sign is an act of confession, a declaration of belonging to the covenantal group, often practiced in foreign, if not hostile surroundings. It is practiced once in relation to each male individual: "This is my covenant, which you shall keep, between me and you and your descendants after you: Every male among you shall be circumcised" (Genesis 17:10).

The central covenant relationship is granted to Israel alone, the descendants of Jacob's twelve sons. It is sealed in the encounter between Israel and the Lord at Mount Sinai. Now their God is known to them by his proper name—a name to be guarded carefully from misuse. To this intimate relationship corresponds a sacramental sign which is enacted every week—the observance of the Sabbath:

> . . . the Lord said to Moses, "Say to the people of Israel, 'You shall keep my sabbaths, for this is a sign between me and you throughout your generations. . . Wherefore the people of Israel shall keep the sabbath, observing the sabbath throughout their generations, as a perpetual covenant. It is a sign for ever between me and the people of Israel. . . ." (Exod. 31:12-13, 16-17)

Three covenant dispensations, three revelations of the divine name, three covenantal signs: successive and concentric in relation to each other—an impressively comprehensive understanding of the covenant indeed! Here, both the particularity of Israel and the universality of God's will are brought together into creative tension. This covenantal concept was bequeathed to many generations in synagogue and church. It highlights rather than solves the question: covenant—how universal?

c. How Spiritual?

Another issue for the understanding of the covenant emerged clearly during the Babylonian exile. It had been long in the making; we already observed it in some of the prophets who spoke before the exile. It came to a head in the words of Jeremiah. He observed that his contemporaries had externalized the ancient covenant and its observances. Thus Jeremiah calls for "the circumcision of the heart" and indicates that this is the real issue of the rite.

> For thus says the Lord to the men of Judah and to the inhabitants of Jerusalem: "Break up your fallow ground, and sow not among thorns. Circumcise yourselves to the Lord, remove the foreskin of your hearts, O men of Judah and inhabitants of Jerusalem; lest my wrath go forth like fire, and burn with none to quench it, because of the evil of your doings." (Jer. 4:3-4)

It is evident that Jeremiah does not oppose the observance of the rite of circumcision as a covenantal act. What he demands is that the people's internal attitude correspond to the observance of the rite so that it reflects both reality and demands of the covenant relationship. We may describe this emphasis as an internalization of the covenant; we could equally speak of the spiritualization of the idea of the covenant (compare further Jeremiah 9:25-26).

Emphasis on both internal and external observance of the covenantal demands prepared ancient Israel for life in the exile. At that time many of the familiar, inherited external observances were no longer possible. Still, when they were far from their land and temple, they prayed in the direction of the temple, thus indicating that they were still oriented toward the land that once was their God-given home. This is also illustrated in the Book of Daniel where the hero of the stories, Daniel, is described as singularly faithful in exile. He is portrayed as one who regularly prays toward Jerusalem. He does so in the privacy of his house where he has windows in his upper chamber "open toward Jerusalem." (See Daniel 6:10.)

The spiritualization of the cult was a necessity in the situation of exile. We readily understand the prayers of the Psalmist: "Let my prayer be counted as incense before thee, and the lifting up of my hands as an evening sacrifice!" (Psalm 141:2). In the exile, when the burning of incense and the evening sacrifice could not be offered, the prayers and gestures which accompanied the rites became their substitutes.

On the whole, external and internal observance of the demands of the covenant were not often pitted against each other in ancient Israel. But it must be stressed that the claims of the covenant do not allow any sphere of life, whether on the individual or the corporate plane, to remain exempt. Thus Jeremiah or the Deuteronomic preachers stress wholehearted observance of the covenant whenever life—communal and individual, religious and secular—exhausts itself in the routine performance of rites and ceremonies. This is well shown by Jeremiah's reproach of those who relied all too readily, all too superficially, on the presence of the Lord in the temple: "Do not trust in these deceptive words: 'This is the temple of the Lord, the temple of the Lord, the temple of the Lord' " (Jer. 7:4).

The internalization of the covenant means truly amending one's ways and doings and executing justice (Jeremiah 7:5). The Deuteronomic writers put it this way:

> The Lord your God will circumcise your heart and the heart of your offspring, so that you will love the Lord your God with all your heart and with all your soul, that you may live. (Deut. 30:6)

d. How Enduring?

In the words of the later prophets, election and covenant are prominent themes. Jeremiah, Ezekiel, and Isaiah of Babylon (Isaiah 40-55) cannot be understood without them, and yet something new appears in the way they speak of the inherited traditions of Israel. These prophets are not primarily interested in the traditions as patterns of God's action in the past, but view them as the shape which God's *future* action will take. They are convinced that Israel's covenant relationship as it had existed from days of old is broken (Jeremiah 31:32, Ezekiel 44:7). Israel's disobedience led, as the prophets Amos and Hosea had already affirmed, to the disasters of 722 B.C.–the destruction of the kingdom of Israel and the exile of its elite. Later prophets spoke of the destruction of the kingdom of Judah with its capital, Jerusalem, and of the Babylonian exile for the Judean elite.

Yet in the despair of the Babylonian exile--when God's history with his people seems to have come to an end and when the covenant and its blessings seem irrevocably lost–in this deepest crisis of Israel's history, prophets rise and speak of a new beginning. Jeremiah says that the Lord will grant a new covenant:

> Behold, the days are coming, says the Lord, when I will make a new covenant with the house of Israel and the house of Judah, not like the covenant which I made with their fathers. . . . But this is the covenant which I will make . . .: I will put my law within them, and I will write it upon their hearts; and I will be their God, and they shall be my people. (Jer. 31:31-33)

Ezekiel speaks of new beginnings in similar terms. The goal of the new divine initiative is the full realization of the covenant relationship between God and his people. This is evident in the use of the covenant formula by Ezekiel: "You shall be my people, and I will be your God" (Ezekiel 36:28).

Isaiah of Babylon speaks in a similar vein of a new exodus. It will be like the exodus from Egypt, yet more glorious (Isaiah 48:20, 49:9-12). He also speaks of a rebuilt Jerusalem (Isaiah 49:14-18, 52:8). God's covenant with David shall be renewed, and transferred to the whole nation as the descendants of David (Isaiah 55:3, cf. Amos 9:11). Ezekiel goes still farther and speaks of a new creation; he does so in his vision of the valley of dry bones (Ezekiel 37:1-14). All these prophets agree that the new covenant which God is shaping is patterned after his acts of salvation in the past, yet will far surpass them. Isaiah of Babylon can even exhort his listeners to forget "the former things," that is, God's mighty deeds of the past (Isaiah 43:18).

Thus the prophets of the Babylonian exile show themselves rooted in the traditions of election and covenant. What is new is the way in which they draw Israel's eyes away from the past and direct them to the future.

Now the covenant is not a matter of what was, but of what is to be. These prophetic expectations were preserved by prophetic disciples and so became a force in the history of both the early synagogue and the early church. Small wonder that the early church, believing the new covenant had been established in Jesus' coming, quoted these ancient words of prophetic expectation! In fact, they provided many Christians with the key to understanding Jesus' words.

The prophetic expectation of a new covenant contrasts starkly with emphasis on the eternity of the covenant as set forth in priestly circles. In the cultic covenant texts of the Pentateuch we hear several times that the covenant dispensations which God granted are valid forever. All of creation is included, and all time is encompassed. God's covenant once set up cannot be abrogated—it is eternal!

What we encounter here is the most crucial tension in the understanding of the covenant in ancient Israel. Does the radical break caused by the exile mean that now God's covenant of old is a matter of the past? With the exilic prophets must one look forward to a new covenant dispensation? Some prophetic voices answer yes. Or can one affirm that God's covenant of old bridges even the dark chasm of the exile, and so is promise of God's future presence with Israel? Priestly voices whom we hear in the Pentateuch and also in the Chronicler answer yes.

Under the impact of Jesus' word and work, the tension between the old covenant (which is eternal) and the expected new covenant (which supersedes the old) becomes the basis for two rival claims on the sacred tradition of ancient Israel. Many early Christians see in Jesus the initiator of the new covenant of which prophetic voices (now enshrined in the Hebrew Scriptures) spoke. Hence they will claim for Jesus the honor and place given to the one who initiated the covenant of old. In other words, Jesus is a new Moses and the mediator of a new covenant. On the other hand, Jewish-Christian groups and early rabbinic teachers will maintain that God's covenant once given cannot be abrogated. They believe that it stands forever. Any abrogation of it through the setting up of a new covenant, they maintain, is a betrayal of the ancient tradition.

Here an unfortunate split happens in the understanding of the covenant:

---

both synagogue and church claim the covenant of old for themselves. The synagogue

does so by asserting the unbroken continuance of the covenant, while for the church what has happened in Jesus is the initiation of the new covenant.

5.

COVENANT ETERNAL- THE SYNAGOGUE

The centuries before the coming of Jesus are, to some extent, shrouded in darkness. We do not have enough writings from post-exilic Judaism to show fully how Jewish groups in that period transmitted their legacy and interpreted it afresh. However, we do have many writings from the last two centuries B.C. which give full accounts of particular Jewish groups such as the Pharisees, the followers of the Maccabees, or the people of the Dead Sea Scrolls.

The main collection is the Old Testament Apocrypha which is found in some modern Bible editions as an appendix to the Old Testament. Outstanding are Jesus ben Sira (Sirach), a collection of proverbs and discourses coming from the beginning of the second century B.C., and the Wisdom of Solomon, which comes from the different setting of Greek-speaking Jews in metropolitan Alexandria in the last century B.C. We further mention the First and Second Books of the Maccabees, which give us accounts from different perspectives of the uprising of the Maccabeans, their success, and the subsequent founding of an independent Israel in the second half of the second century B.C.

We must also mention the Dead Sea Scrolls, discovered in the late 1940s in caves near the northern end of the Dead Sea. These writings have thrown much light on a fascinating though unique and isolated sectarian group of Intertestamental Judaism. In addition, we have the translation of the Old Testament into Greek made in the last centuries B.C. It transmitted the Jewish religious heritage as enshrined in the Law and the Prophets and the Writings to the much larger, more comprehensive forum of the Hellenistic world where Greek was spoken. Finally, reference must be made to early rabbinic writings such as the Sayings of the Fathers

(Pirke Aboth). It is a tractate of the Mishnah, the collection of Jewish ethical lore, compiled A.D. 200. Here we find reflected in an admirable way the thinking and feeling of the synagogue and of Jewish groups in the first two centuries of our era. All these writings are important because the idea of covenant is found in them.

The Hebrew word which, in the Old Testament versions, is commonly translated with the English word *covenant* was rendered into Greek by a term which does justice to the Hebrew original only to a certain extent. It is a divergence known to translators; they often find that a word in one language is not identical with a word in another language. It is noteworthy that these translators rendered the Hebrew "covenant" with a Greek word which stressed more its legal aspect, its fixed contractual quality, and less the mutuality of the relationship which the Hebrew term implied. For Greek-speaking Jews the covenant of old became more and more the codification of the divine will given at Mount Sinai through Moses. (Compare Exodus 34:27-28, Deuteronomy 4:13.) It was now a written code!

The tendency to narrow the Old Testament covenant to a legal document can be observed in the passage penned at the beginning of the second century B.C. by an ancient Israelite scholar and wise man, Jesus ben Sira (Sirach) from whom we have a book of proverbs by the same name.

In chapter 39:1-11 we encounter an instructive description of the scripture scholar of that time. He "devotes himself to the study of the law of the Most High," he "will seek out the wisdom of all the ancients, and will be concerned with prophecies; he will preserve the discourse of notable men and penetrate the subtleties of parables; he will seek out the hidden meanings of proverbs and be at home with the obscurities of parables." This description of the ideal scripture student stresses that he is able to "reveal instruction in his teaching, and will glory in the law of the Lord's covenant" (Jesus ben Sira 39:1-3, 8). It is evident that here the Lord's covenant is represented through the law which, in turn, is seen as the basic content of the covenant.

This is also well illustrated in a poem that praises wisdom, found in Jesus ben Sira, chapter 24. Here we find "wisdom" described in glowing terms, but are told at the end of the poem that "all this is the book of the covenant of the Most High God, the law which Moses commanded us as an inheritance for the congregations of Jacob" (24: 23). Here again the covenant is defined almost as a book, something that is codified and granted to

Israel once for all. Israel responds to God's covenant by its "delight . . . in the law of the Lord, and on his law he meditates day and night" (Psalm 1:2; compare Psalm 119 which through some 176 verses extols "the law of the Lord").

This is confirmed by the story of the uprising of the first Maccabees in 168 B.C. Their possession of "the book of the covenant" and the adherence "to the law" is reason for being condemned by a Gentile king who seeks to suppress the Jews and their religion. We find the story of the uprising against the Hellenistic oppressors described briefly in 1 Maccabees 1: 56-57 (RSV):

> The books of the law which they found they tore to pieces and burned with fire. Where the book of the covenant was found in the possession of any one, or if any one adhered to the law, the decree of the king condemned him to death.

This is a telling commentary on the way in which life in the covenant and adherence to the law had become synonymous–an understandable but one-sided understanding of what covenant is.

The Dead Sea Scrolls must be discussed briefly. In the major writings preserved and edited so far, the word "covenant" occurs at least 115 times! This Jewish splinter group lived a solitary life in a monastery-like settlement near the northern end of the Dead Sea from approximately 150 B.C. to A.D. 73, when the Roman armies destroyed their buildings. The sectaries were evidently able to save their treasured library by hiding the scrolls in nearby caves where they remained undiscovered until 1947.

These people understood themselves as the people of the covenant, as the faithful remnant–in fact, the only remnant of Israel true to the covenant. Everybody who joined the community pledged himself "freely by a binding oath to return with all his heart and soul to all that has been revealed to the Zadokite priests, who are the keepers of the covenant. . . ." Each member of the community "enters into the covenant and separates himself from all the men of falsehood who live in unrighteousness and who are not reckoned (to stand) in the covenant" (Community Rule, column 5). It is clear that for the people of the Dead Sea Scrolls, the covenant once made with Israel is eternal. However, almost all Jews have forsaken that covenant and only those who have joined this small group in exile at the northern end of the Dead Sea are those who have fully reentered the eternal covenant. Only they uphold and continue that covenant now.

In early Rabbinic Judaism this same notion is alive, too. Here it can be said in a midrash (an interpretation) of the book of Exodus that there is no covenant except the law. The identification of the covenant with the written law is clear. As such it is token and sign of God's presence within and will for the Israel of the synagogue. It is, of course, eternal and not to be abrogated. Usually it is understood to refer to the rite of circumcision which initiates the male Israelite into the covenant (Genesis 17:10); at times it is formulated in opposition to a Christian interpretation of Jeremiah 31:31-34 according to which the new covenant is interpreted as radical abrogation of the covenant of old.

The view of Rabbinic Judaism is well-expressed in the Mishnah tractate "Sayings of the Fathers." There we read:

> Moses received the Torah from Sinai and delivered it to Joshua, and Joshua to the elders, and the elders to the prophets, and the prophets delivered it to the men of the Great Synagogue. (Pirke Aboth 1:1a)

The men of the Great Synagogue are a legendary group of people who are believed to have established post-exilic Judaism; thus they are "the fathers" of the synagogue as it persisted through the ages. Emphasis on the continuity of God's revelation in the law is important here. It is passed from generation to generation; it is not to be abrogated, it is eternal, it endures forever. We note the stress on the eternity of God's self-revelation in the law. Already encountered in the priestly writings of the Pentateuch, this understanding of the covenant provided the basis for the ongoing life of Jewish groups in the humble and humbling conditions of exile and dispersion.

6.

NEW COVENANT-THE CHURCH

Word and notion of covenant do not occur as often in the New Testament as one would expect. Of the thirty-three occurrences, seven are quotes of Old Testament texts in which the word "covenant" occurs. All the covenant texts can be divided into three groups: (1) several important passages in the writings of the Apostle Paul; (2) in the Letter to the Hebrews; and (3) in the Synoptic Gospels (Matthew, Mark, and Luke) where the idea of covenant is connected with the institution of the Lord's Supper.

In the Christian churches even before the Apostle Paul, the notion of a new covenant was current. This is evident in the liturgy of the Lord's Supper which the apostle said had been transmitted to him. He quotes it in 1 Corinthians 11:23-25:

> For I received from the Lord what I also delivered to you, that the Lord Jesus on the night when he was betrayed . . . "This cup is the new covenant in my blood."

What happened in Jesus' death is oriented toward the Christian congregation and makes them into the new people of God. This notion is also important for Paul himself (see 2 Corinthians 3:6-8, 14; Galatians 4:24, and below) and to the author of the Letter to the Hebrews (see 8:8, 9:15, 12:24), who in Hebrews 8:10-11 quotes at length from Jeremiah 31:31-34, which is the promise of the new covenant made to the people of Israel.

As a curiosity we note that the covenant idea plays a special role in the apocryphal Letter of Barnabas. This early Christian writing was not accepted into the canon of the New Testament, but nevertheless was read in some early Christian circles and held in great respect. There the covenant idea appears in a peculiar interpretation, showing an almost arrogant attitude of some early Christians. The author argues that the people of ancient Israel never really were in a covenant relationship with God because their idolatry never allowed them to be in the covenant. Hence, there is no such thing as a new covenant, because there is only the one covenant which was from the beginning intended for the Christian church!

As for the Apostle Paul, it is evident that he came to be a follower of Jesus by way of a radical break with his past: the zealous Pharisee who persecuted Christian congregations turned into an ambassador of Christ. Soon he was to shape significantly the witness and work of the early churches. (See Philippians 3:4-7 for Paul's own description of his past in relation to his present.)

It is small wonder that Paul developed his theology in the light of this radical break and that he delighted in the radical contrasts, for instance, between what was and what is now, between the old and the new, between flesh and the spirit (compare Romans 7:1-25, 2 Corinthians 5:17). These radical contrasts, typical for Paul's theology, have made this apostle the most sharply profiled one among the writers of the New Testament. However, this sharp either-or of Paul has set the tone for many Christians. For better or for worse they exclusively fasten onto these radical antitheses.

Also, the concept of the covenant is pressed by Paul into this mold. For instance, in 2 Corinthians 3:4-6 Paul bases his argument on the notion of a new covenant as found in Jeremiah 31:31-34. Then he claims that what has happened in Christ is the inauguration of the new covenant. He says this when he has to defend himself against people who accuse him of being underhanded and of little authority. For him, Christ "has qualified us to be ministers of a new covenant, not in a written code but in the Spirit; for the written code kills, but the Spirit gives life" (2 Corinthians 3:6). Paul sets forth not only the contrast between an old covenant and a new covenant, but also between a written code and the work of the Spirit. For Paul, brought up in the Judaism of his period, the covenant is identical with the law. The law, on the other hand, he claims to have been both fulfilled and abrogated in Christ (Romans 10:5). Here he evidently stands in sharp contrast to the Judaism which had nurtured him. There the law is the supreme token and symbol of God's covenant relationship with Israel. Paul argues against his Jewish past and seeks to get hold of who he is as a follower of Jesus in light of a radical contrast. There is no doubt that passages such as Jereminah 31:31-34, which speak of a new covenant and were part of the sacred writings of the synagogue, play an important role in supporting, if not evoking Paul's radical argument. In fact, Paul goes further and argues in the same chapter that the Jews are unable to recognize the splendor, the superiority of the most recent and new covenant. He says that whenever the Jews read (the Scripture of) the old covenant, their faces are veiled; they are not able to see the splendor radiating from the new covenant and surpassing the old covenant.

For Paul the new covenant dispensation stands in a line with the series of covenant dispensations which he knows from the Old Testament; in Romans 9:4 he acknowledges several of them. Paul thinks in terms of periods of history. The old period under the custodian's restraint lies in the past. The man who once held the position of a slave under the law has been set free to be no longer a ward; now he has the rights of a son (Galatians 3:23-4:7). The old covenant, Paul claims, led to death and condemnation. It has now faded away and has been replaced by the new covenant with its ministrations of the spirit and of righteousness forever (2 Corinthians 3:1-12).

The most notable feature of Paul's understanding of the new covenant is that it is a covenant initiated by and born of the Spirit. He says "where the Spirit of the Lord is, there is freedom" (2 Corinthians 3:17). It is this notion of freedom which fills and gives substance to the Pauline understanding of the new covenant (Galatians 5:1, 4:6; Romans 8:15).

For the writer of the Letter to the Hebrews the idea of the new covenant is equally important. In fact, he is the only one of the New Testament writers who quotes Jeremiah 31:31-34 in full (Hebrews 8:8-12). He then continues and says, "In speaking of a new covenant he (God) treats the first as obsolete. And what is becoming obsolete and growing old is ready to vanish away" (8:13). He proceeds to discuss extensively the contrast between the old and the new covenant, showing that the new covenant corresponds to the old covenant, yet exceeds and supersedes it.

It is clear, however, that in distinction to Paul and Jeremiah he sees both old and new covenant as cultic institutions; they have been granted by God and are ritually ordered through priestly ministrations in order to effect forgiveness of sins, atonement, and purification. The new covenant is the place where the heavenly high priest, Jesus, officiates–a high priest who sacrifices himself and so is almost literally the fulfillment of the earlier priesthood, the priesthood of the old covenant which was earthbound. Those priestly ministrations were only a shadow of the things to come, the heavenly things (Hebrews 8:5). Thus, his argument is well summarized when he speaks of Christ as "the mediator of a new covenant" (Hebrews 9:15).

The early church celebrated the Lord's Supper on Sunday. This joint meal is the center of Christian communal life and worship. It fits in with the custom of Jewish groups to eat their meals together. It begins with the breaking of the bread and concludes with the passing of the cup of wine. Such meals are attested also in the Dead Sea Scrolls. For the early Christians, the Lord's Supper was the continuation of this meal fellowship which the disciples had had with the earthly Jesus. The last meal Jesus ate with his followers set the pattern for the service of the common meal after Jesus' death and resurrection. Small wonder that the Apostle Paul can quote to the Corinthian congregation as old tradition the story of the institution of the Lord's Supper when he says:

> I received from the Lord what I also delivered to you, that the Lord Jesus on the night when he was betrayed took bread, and when he had given thanks, he broke it, and said, "This is my body which is (broken) for you. Do this in remembrance of me." In the same way also the cup, after supper, saying, "This cup is the new covenant in my blood. Do this, as often as you drink it, in remembrance of me." For as often as you eat this bread and drink the cup, you proclaim the Lord's death until he comes. (1 Cor. 11:23-26)

Paul quotes this inherited liturgy in order to reject the Corinthians' practice of making this communal meal one in which everyone eats whatever he or she has, without waiting for others. Thus they show no regard to the community which, after all, manifests itself in the communal meal (compare 1 Corinthians 11:33-34). In other words, the common meal establishes full and true communion and community among those who eat together, and in this way manifests the new covenant into which their following Jesus has brought them.

Also in the Synoptic Gospels the words of the institution of the Lord's Supper are connected with the concept of the covenant (Mark 14:22-25; Matthew 26:26-29; Luke 22:15-20). The exact wording varies from evangelist to evangelist. Suffice it to say that these words were formulated in Christian tradition on the basis both of Jeremiah 31:31-34 (where the new covenant is promised as forgiveness of sins) and the ancient story of the concluding of the covenant with the Israelites at Mount Sinai. There the covenant was sealed in a communal meal and with a rite carried out by Moses when he took the blood of sacrifices, threw it on the people, and said, "Behold the blood of the covenant which the Lord has made with you in accordance with all these words" (Exodus 24:1-11).

To reiterate: in the three groups of New Testament passages where the concept of covenant is important, its interpretation as a *new* covenant is central. That new covenant is patterned after the covenant of old. It either fulfills or supplants the old covenant. The goal of the newly initiated covenant is in keeping with the goal of the covenants instituted of old in ancient Israel: either freedom (2 Corinthians 3:6-8, 17-19); brotherly or sisterly communion with others bound into the same covenant (1 Corinthians 11:23-26, 33-34); or the perfect atonement once for all wrought and completed through Christ's ministry (Hebrews 9:15). In all cases the purpose and aim of the newly inaugurated covenant are those of the covenants concluded with Israel long ago. It was classically set forth in the formula "You shall be my people, and I will be your God" as said by the divine covenant partner to the Israelites (Ezekiel 36:28).

In the centuries which followed, the notion of the covenant became enshrined both in the Old and New Testament. As far as the church was concerned, it even gave the name to its sacred scripture: the Latin word *testamentum* is a rendering of the Greek and Hebrews words for *covenant.* It moved into English in the New Testament. In the synagogue the Hebrew scriptures are named the Law, the Prophets, and the Writings; their Christian name the Old Testament is, of course, not acceptable to Jewish faith. On the whole, though, neither the synagogue nor the church concerned themselves much in the first centuries of our era with the pattern of covenant; it lay dormant in the scriptures. Yet it also lay there ready at hand for those Christians and Jews who returned to their sources as found in Sacred Scripture. Covenant offered itself more than once as an interpretive category for new situations and new challenges. Sometimes the covenant idea indirectly influenced secular cultural and political life as well, especially when in the Christian tradition the secular political realm and the spiritual religious sphere overlapped or altogether merged.

In addition covenant was an important social and religious model for ancient Israel and for the early Christians. It came to structure oral and written traditions enshrined later in the Old Testament and in the New Testament. It was a flexible pattern of ordering both human and divine-human relationships. Covenant is a partnership which creates a sphere in which the partners became like blood brothers and sisters.

The covenant was capable of being hierarchically or cultically centered in king or priest. By some it was seen as eternal, by others as capable of being broken and having to be renewed. Sometimes its spiritual quality was stressed; at other times, its external signs. Sometimes it was understood to be exclusive; at other times, to be inclusive. It was spiritualized and radicalized, and by the same token despatialized and detemporalized, so that *covenant* could be any place, any time. It was a covenant which could not be safely relegated to the past. The Deuteronomic preachers remind their hearers that the covenant is, and will always remain, a reality here and now, any time, any place:

> The Lord our God made a covenant with us in Horeb. Not with our fathers did the Lord make this covenant, but with us, who are all of us here alive this day. (Deut. 5:2-3)

PART TWO

COVENANT--THE IMPACT OF A MOTIF

Rosemary Radford Ruether

7.

RELIGIOUS COMMUNITIES AS COVENANTED COMMUNITIES: REFORM AND RENEWAL IN THE COVENANT

The idea of the Church as a new or renewed covenant is fundamental to the meaning of the Christian Church. Christianity probably developed this idea parallel to other types of messianic sectarian Judaism, such as the Covenanters of the Dead Sea Scroll community. The Church is seen as the remnant or the True Israel which God has gathered out into the Wilderness. The relationship of the believer to the covenanted community is not one of natural inheritance, but one of conversion and voluntary association. The community of the New Covenant is one that gathers out and over against ordinary evil society. It opposes, too, that established religion which has made its peace too easily with evil, worldly society. The new covenanters are those who dedicate themselves anew to life in God's commandments. They expect soon the appearance of the final messianic crises of history.

In the fourth century A.D. these themes tended to disappear from the center of the Christian concept of the Church. At that time the Church lost its sense of apocalyptic tension with the world and was institutionalized within a Christianized Roman empire. These new covenant themes belong to a more sectarian, voluntarist and apocalyptic sense of the Church. They often appear in puritanical reform movements that criticize the mainstream church's tendency to accommodate itself to the norms of society. Groups like Montanists, Novatianists, and Donatists (sectarian Christian groups from the second to fourth centuries) represented this stricter concept of the Church.

To some extent, monastic communities also preserved within the larger institutionalized Church the option of a "higher" and more rigorous voluntary community. One joined such a group as an adult as an act of conversion to the more committed life in accordance with God's commands of perfection. The rule of the religious community shows that the monastic order is a group which covenants together to live a common life. The monk or nun, in taking his or her vows, assents to this compact to live under a common discipline in accordance with agreed-upon rules. These rules govern the ordinary details of polity, economic labor, and distribution, and also guide the pursuit of virtue and obedience to God within the common life. However, the term "covenant" is not generally used for this idea of common life in monastic communities. It is assumed that the New Covenant is one established by Christ as the common framework within which all Christians live. Monks and nuns are merely living out this covenant in a particularly conscious and rigorous way.

The term covenant as a way of defining the Church came back into special attention with the Reformation. The Reformed, especially the Zwinglian tradition, and the Anabaptists made special use of the concept of the covenant. But each used this concept in distinct and different ways. The Reformed tradition did not use "covenant" to designate the constitution of their Church polity itself. Rather they used it (contrary to the Anabaptist view) to defend the inheritance of the covenant of grace by the children of the Community.

Reminding us of the Old Testament covenant, Christ has established a historical covenanted people through his death and resurrection. God has chosen the numbers of his elect people long before we could respond to this election. Baptism is the sign of the new covenant, as circumcision was the sign of the old. According to the Reformed tradition, all children born into the Christian community can be presumed to have inherited at least the outward context of the community of the new covenant and thus can be baptized as infants as the expression of this inheritance. They will show through their response to Christian nurture in the church and family whether they are, in fact, among the invisible band of God's elect. With this reasoning the Reformed tradition defended their continued use of infant baptism against the Anabaptist insistence on believer's baptism.

The Anabaptists took a very different view, and developed a quite distinct use of the term "covenant" in their understanding of the Church. For the Anabaptists, membership in the Church could not be inherited by birth in the Christian family or community. They maintained that the Church which had merged with society and the state at the time of Constantine was a false and fallen Church. It had lost the true principle of ecclesiastical government. The true Church, they said, is a church separated from the world and conformed to the Spirit of Christ. For Anabaptists this meant a break with the territorial parish of the established church. All ties between church and state must be broken. The Church was to receive no support from the state and accept no coercion from the state upon its doctrine or membership.

Separation also meant certain breaks with the lifestyle of the world. In some cases frivolous possessions and gaudy clothes were rejected in favor of the plain style of dress, speech and life. Military office and often civil office were rejected because such functions involved the use of the power of the sword—something Anabaptists did not think was appropriate for Christians. More radical Anabaptist communities moved out of towns into rural areas where they could practice their ideals of life apart from the distractions of the "world." Sometimes, as with the Hutterites, this involved the adoption of a communism of property and production where all but the most immediate possessions were held in common.

The essence of the Anabaptist concept of the Church is that of a voluntary community gathered, through adult or believer's conversion, into an intimate fellowship of shared faith and commitment. There is no place for passive Christians in this scheme. All who enter the Church do so as a personal decision of faith with a high level of conscious commitment. All can then be prepared to be ministers, evangelists, and even martyrs if need be. Committed Christians of this type are prepared to dedicate their whole beings to a transformed lifestyle involving great and even ultimate sacrifices.

It is in the context of this understanding of the believer's Church that Anabaptists use the term "covenant" as an essential element of their understanding of Church polity. Covenant means the relationship of forgiveness and salvation established by Christ between God and the believer. It also means the believer's voluntary entrance into that covenant with God. This covenant with God establishes, at the same time, a covenant between believers themselves by which they enter consciously into an agreement to live in a committed, disciplined, and loving fellowship with each other. This covenant involves a willingness to abide by rigorous rules of common life and accept the godly admonitions of communal discipline.

Melchior Hoffman, one of the thinkers of the first generation of Anabaptism, speaks of the covenanted community ecstatically as a marriage contract between the Church and Christ:

> And now in this final age the true apostolic emissaries of the Lord Jesus Christ will gather the elect flock and call it through the gospel and lead the Bride of the Lord into the spiritual wilderness, betroth and covenant her through baptism to the Lord. Thus also St. Paul (II Cor. 11:2)

> had betrothed the Church of Corinth to the Lord as a virgin to her husband and bound it under the covenant.[1]

The New England Congregationalists inherited and fused elements of both the Calvinist and Anabaptist concepts of covenant. Like the Reformed theologians, they stressed the historic covenant of grace. God throughout ages past and continuing to the present generation has bound himself to a special covenant with his elect people. This covenant is wholly the work of God's grace. This covenant of grace can neither be initiated nor ultimately broken by sinful humanity. It represents the specific plan of God for electing and covenanting to himself those whom he has chosen to bring into the fulfillment of the promises of salvation. These people God governs not only with special grace, but also with special chastisement, to form them into a disciplined and godly people.

However, in addition to this emphasis on the historic and gracious nature of the covenant, New England Congregationalists took over from Anabaptism the concept of covenant as a voluntary pact between church members to enter into a common fellowship and church government together. The Mayflower compact extended this idea of covenant to include civil society. The signers of the Mayflower pact, who included non-Church members, pledged themselves to found a godly commonwealth. This was anticipated by the Anabaptist understanding of the Church as a disciplined community whose rules covered the whole of the lives of believers.

The covenantal idea of the Church assumes rigorous standards of Church membership, including personal experience of conversion. The covenant of the Salem community in 1629 was established with this brief statement of their common contract:

> We covenant with the Lord and with one another and do bind ourselves in the presence of God to walk together in all his ways, according as he is pleased to reveal himself unto us in his Blessed word of truth.[2]

All who desired to unite with the Salem group on the basis of this covenant were examined in regard to their knowledge of the principles of religion, their personal experience of the grace of conversion, and godly conduct in their daily lives. Only those who passed these tests without serious reproach were admitted as members of the Church. Soon a large number of colonists found themselves outside the Church covenant! Difficulties particularly arose in the admission of members' children who had not yet experienced personal conversion. This led finally in 1665 to the formation of the half-way covenant whereby children of the baptized could be admitted to membership on the basis of the belief of their parents.

The strength of the covenantal idea of the Church lies in its stress on active faith and commitment of each member.

This makes covenanted ideas of the Church arise again and again in time of renewal when there is a stress on the active choice, rather than the passive inheritance of Church membership. Yet by the same token, the weakness of such intentional communities lies in the difficulties of perpetuating them historically. Monastic communities had solved this problem by making themselves a special and "higher option" within the larger church. Those already baptized could choose this as an adult decision. But those who try to perpetuate the intentional community by natural propagation often find the second generation apathetic toward the concerns that led their parents to their original commitment.

Voluntary or intentional communities cannot perpetuate themselves by historical inheritance, but only by the continual renewal of their spirit. This means that the voluntary idea of community arises continually in times of tension with the old order of society and church to express the renewed vision of committed Christian life. Such intentional communities often last for only a generation or less. Those who manage to last much longer—such as the Hutterite communities, which have a continuous history since the sixteenth-century Reformation—do so by practicing a rigid segregation from the life style of society around them. They try to shield the children from alternative options. Other communities, which originate in the believer's concept of the church, gradually take on the aspects of historical churches. They no longer demand personal conversion and high levels of commitment for church membership. Nevertheless the Spirit has proved fertile in generating continual expressions of the committed community. Perhaps no country has seen so many forms of intentional community ebb and flow across its land as the United States.

In America, religious communalism comes down from various streams of left-wing Protestantism: Hutterites, Mennonites and Amish, German sectarian movements of the seventeenth-century pietist revival, and English radical sects such as the Shakers are among these. The Moravian Brethren formed several communities in Pennsylvania and North

Carolina. Ascetic sects, like the German Baptist community of Ephrata, Pennsylvania, imitated the severe habits of a medieval cloister. Other intentional communities arose from secular socialist inspiration, such as the Owenites of New Harmony, Indiana, and the short-lived Fourierite communities. The New England transcendentalists planted several colonies for short periods. The radical community of the Oneida Perfectionists in upstate New York mingled the secular idea of genetic breeding with the Christian concept of the redeemed millennial Church.[3]

The 1830s-70s were the peak of these earlier efforts at founding communal societies in America. By the end of the century many of these communities had died out or survived only in remnants. The 1920s also saw some renewed efforts at communal experimentation, such as the Catholic Worker movement. But the latter half of the 1960s, with its diverse movements of religious and social dissent, saw the greatest resurgence of this impulse toward community-building. Americans have formed communities out of a variety of needs. Urban communes served short-term needs of survival for those trying to work out philosophies of life. Disgust with consumer society took many small groups back to the land to recover a sense of basic necessities. The ecological consciousness, with its warnings against the dangerous destructiveness of modern artificial technology, brought a new earnestness to this effort.

Ecological New Covenanters experience the sense of the broken covenant, not only between human and human, and between humanity and God, but also in destructive relations between humanity and *nature.* This is the theme which is expressed so powerfully in prophetic passages in the Old Testament, especially Isaiah 24:4-6:

> The earth mourns and withers, the world languishes and withers; the heavens languish together with the earth.
>
> The earth lies polluted under its inhabitants; for they have transgressed the laws, violated the statutes, broken the everlasting covenant.
>
> Therefore a curse devours the earth, and its inhabitants suffer for their guilt.

The Old Testament understanding of covenant included not only the historic covenant of God with Abraham and Moses, but also the creational covenant by which God established the foundations of the earth and the heavens. The creational covenant was also a theme maintained in the Reformation renewal of the covenant concept. But, in practice, it was overshadowed by the prevailing theology of man's natural depravity. A new covenant of grace had to be established through Christ.

The rapid spread of modern technological civilization has shown us our fragility. Our historical civilization and even the very tissue of our biological survival in the environment of soil, water, air, plants and animals is endangered. Nature, through human technology, itself becomes historical. It too enters into the history of human fallenness. This brings before us a renewed sense of the Old Testament vision. Sinfulness breaks not only the compacts with God and with society, but with nature as well. Likewise the renewed covenant with God and with each other must also be a renewal of our covenant with nature. We must discover again how to live with the earth and share its goods with one another in a way that nurtures rather than destroys its capacities for regeneration. It is somewhat along these lines that intentional communities in the 1960s and 70s have made the commitment to ecological living an important part of their agenda.

One of the basic tensions between the concept of the intentional community and the mainstream Church is the conflict between two goals of church life: the impulse to turn inward in a highly selective, closed community in pursuit of perfection, and the impulse to remain open and at the service of a still unredeemed world. Many of the intentional communities being founded in the 1960s sought to resolve that tension by distinguishing these two purposes of their communities. On the one hand, the group covenants together to live under common discipline that expresses ideals of life. But they also constitute themselves as service communities to the larger world—as task forces, training centers, or ministers to the needs of the poor around them. The Philadelphia Life Community belongs to this type of intentional community. It has both an inward and an outward purpose. It not only comprises a group of communities who live together, but also runs training sessions in peace action which may draw people to its area. It may even send training groups to many other cities across the country.

The Community for Creative Non-Violence in Washington, D.C. similarly gathers a community which engages in many works of service. Among these are a soup kitchen for the poorest people of the city, a medical aid clinic, a legal defense service, and a peace action center. Its ideas are propagated through lectures and seminars held in the community building. A community printing press allows the members to communicate their visions and concerns. The commitment to poverty and communal living allows a number of people to be freed from the rat-race of jobs to use much of their energies in service to others.

The intentional community, as an expression of the Church, easily becomes ingrown and self-righteous when seen as an end in itself. However, as a provisional community of high commitment to common discipline, which at the same time commits itself to service to others, it may truly be the leaven in the lump of society and the Church. Such communities serve constantly to remind us what the church should really be. They show us what ends of justice and peace a society "under God" should really be serving. As optional service communities within the larger Christian covenant, such groups are freed from having to perpetuate themselves once the spirit is gone. They are also freed to change and develop with the needs and inspirations of the times. Christians who inherit the faith can rediscover the power of living and acting in that faith. So the intentional community functions as the vehicle of renewed commitment which may illuminate and inspire many around it.

8.

MARRIAGE AS A SIGN OF THE COVENANT

In this chapter we consider a somewhat special topic that is not always discussed in relationship to the topic of covenant: marriage as a sign or symbol of the covenant. How does such a symbol affect our view of the covenant between humanity and God? The Church and God? Especially, how does such a sign affect our view of marriage? Marriage is recognized as the basic social unit of society, so to consider it under the topic of covenantal relations says some important things about our view of society. But in the Reformed traditions especially, the family is often considered the basic unit of the Church as well. The symbolic interactions between the Church and the family are important for modeling our view of both the Church and the family. This also affects our images of God-human relations.

The Old Testament uses various images for the covenant. The more common image drawn from the family is that of a relation of a father to a son. The book of Hosea is the most important text where the covenant between God and Israel is imaged as husband and wife or lovers. However, the image is used judgementally. This is probably because the marriage image was one too closely associated with Ba'alism. So the Old Testament takes it over first of all as a way of criticizing the tendency of the Hebrews to continue to worship the old god, Ba'al. But, in the process, Yahweh also claims to be the true "husband" of Israel and so to supplant the old bonds of ba'alistic sacred marriage.

> Behold I will allure her, and bring her into the wilderness and speak tenderly to her.
> And there I will give her vineyards . . . .
> And there she shall answer as in the days of her youth, as at the time

> when she came out of the land of Egypt.
> And in that day, says the Lord, you will call me "My husband" and no longer "My Ba'al."
> For I will remove the names of the Ba'als from her mouth. . . . And I will make for you a covenant on that day with the beasts of the field, the birds of the air, and the creeping things of the ground; and I will abolish the bow, the sword, and war from the land; and I will make you lie down in safety. And I will betroth you to me for ever; I will betroth you to me in righteousness and in justice, in steadfast love, and in mercy. (Hosea 2:14-19)

Here we have a powerful image of the renewal of the covenant as the renewal of the marriage vows between Israel and God. This, in turn, brings about the promised new age of peace, ecological harmony, justice, and righteousness.

The image of marriage continues to be an important one in Christianity as well. In the New Testament it becomes an image of the New Covenant, or the relationship of Christ and the Church. In Ephesians particularly, the nuptial image of Christ and the Church is turned around to become a model for human marriage:

> Wives, be subject to your husbands, as to the Lord. For the husband is the head of the wife as Christ is the head of the Church, his body, and is himself its Savior. As the Church is subject to Christ, so let wives also be subject in everything to their husbands. Husbands, love your wives, as Christ loved the Church and gave himself up for her, that he might sanctify her, having cleansed her by washing of water with the word, that the church might be presented before him in splendor, without spot or wrinkle or any such thing, that she might be holy and without blemish. Even so husbands should love their wives as their own bodies. He who loves his wife loves himself. For no man ever hates his own flesh, but nourishes it and cherishes it, as Christ does the church, because we are members of his body. (Ephesians 5:22-30)

This is a key text for our consideration of the marriage image of the covenant in Christianity. Later on, the author of Ephesians speaks of this marriage image as a "great mystery, and I take it to mean Christ and the Church" (Ephesians 5:32).

There are some peculiar aspects of this image in Christianity. First of all, the image of the Church as bride presented here is not merely the sinful Church or ordinary humanity. Rather it points forward to redeemed or eschatological humanity. The Church as bride of Christ is the representative of the New Jerusalem, cleansed of all sin and totally perfected. The Church as Bride is the eschatological or perfected Church mentioned in the final chapter of Revelation:

> Then I saw a new heaven and a new earth. . . . And I saw the holy city, new Jerusalem, coming down out of heaven from God, prepared as a bride adorned for her husband . . . (Rev. 21:1-2)

This is clearly a strange model after which to pattern human marriage, even as an ideal. How has this image been used in Christian history?

In the early Church and through the Middle Ages, Christianity was influenced by a negative view of sexuality. Marriage came to be seen as a lower form of life. The highest Christian ideal was celibacy. In the cultures influenced by this view, the marriage image of Christ and the Church was not applied very much to real marriage. Rather it was spiritualized and interpreted as a symbol of the mystical marriage of Christ and the soul. The Old Testament erotic poem, The Song of Songs, became the favorite text for this theme of the mystical marriage (between Christ and the soul) for the monks and nuns of the early and medieval Church. But those who read it in this spiritual sense were strictly warned against imagining "carnal thoughts." They should not think that this marriage had anything to do with real marriage in the flesh.

The Reformation was instrumental in setting aside this celibate tradition. It reinstated the family, rather than the monastery, as the basic model for the Church. The father was held up as being—for the family—like the pastor of the church. The family was urged to see itself as a little church both for daily prayer and Scripture reading and for self-examination in the practice of virtue. It was in the Reformed tradition particularly that the nuptial image of the covenant of Christ and the Church was emphasized.

Puritan pulpit literature of the seventeenth century often used the female roles of bride and wife to describe the ideal roles for women. By analogy, roles of bride and wife indicated the ideal relation of all regenerate Christians, male and female, to Christ. Since the elect people, or the Church as a whole, were the bride of Christ, the Church was given a female identity. All regenerate Christians should behave toward Christ as the wife ideally should behave toward her husband. Christians should be completely submissive to Christ, observe his commandments, be eager to please him in every way, be faithful and pure in loyalty to one's true Lord alone. These themes are expounded in writings such as the work of Cotton Mather, the great Puritan preacher, titled *Glorious Espousal; A Brief Essay to Illustrate and Prosecute the Marriage Wherein Our Great Savior Offers To Espouse Himself to the Children of Men* (1719). Christ, in turn, was described as behaving toward the Church as the loving and nurturing husband behaves toward his wife. The marriage relationship of regenerate Christians to Christ was one of total submission of body and will to Him. They received, in return, total assurance of love and safety.

The use of this image of marriage raises a number of questions about ideas of male and female personalities and the nature of marriage. As a model for all Christians, it presupposes that characteristics described as "female" are not limited to women alone. They are capacities of men as well, in that men too are urged to assume these traits in relation to God. Indeed, the traits of submissiveness, obedience, and responsiveness are seen as more Christian than masculine traits. All Christians must learn these traits in order to be open to God's grace. This presumably is easier for women already schooled in these traits in their social role, whereas men would have to break their own social conditioning in order to assume these traits in relation to Christ.

The Christ-Church analogy to marriage makes female traits valuable traits, desirable for all Christians in relation to God. They are also the traits of male and female laity in relation to the clergy as spokespersons for the Word of God. But this same analogy, read back as normative for marriage and social relations, shows its limiting effects for women. The analogy confines women to only one type of personality development: submission, in relation to God, clergy, and husband. Men, on the other hand, are allowed to develop their personalities out of both sides of the analogy. They cultivate female traits in relation to God or divinely ordained authority figures over them. But they can also cultivate the traits of lordship over women and children or servants, for whom they represent God's Word.

This model of social relations and human-divine relations is very hierarchical. Each relation becomes one of dominance and submission. In some of these relations men play the dominant role and in others the submissive. Women are confined to the submissive role alone. Therefore they are excluded not only from a real peer relation with their husbands, but also from the possibility of playing leadership roles in society or the Church. Only in relation to their children do they play authority roles. Here too they are only mediators of the father's authority.

Today women are revolting against this hierarchical, dominance-submission model of marriage of patriarchal society. The Christ-Church analogy is being rejected as a good model for marriage. Not only does this place women in the submissive posture, but there is something unrealistic, even idolatrous, about placing husbands in the place of Christ. The advice to the husband to love his wife as his own body does not mitigate this paternalistic relationship. This deprives women of full personhood and ownership of their own bodies. It elevates males unrealistically as dispensers of grace as if they were God. Our ideal today is the partnership marriage. How might this change our model of marriage as an image of the covenant? How might this also change our idea of the covenant as a relation of humanity and God?

A fully realized partnership marriage would revolutionize our traditional conceptions of what the pact of marriage means. These traditional views still govern, to a large extent, our economic arrangements. This means that they determine the design of our domestic living space in relationship to other institutions, especially the job sectors of society. We still assume that woman's work at home frees the male for exclusive attention to the job, while he maintains the family economically. The removal of farming and crafts from the family means that the males are expected to play much less of a role in parenting than was the case in the pre-industrial, puritan family.

The partnership marriage, by contrast, attempts to divide the roles of jobs and education out in the "world" and parenting more equally between the partners. This means women as well as men contribute to the economic maintenance of the home. Men as well as women are equally parents and houseworkers. Most importantly, it means that men must be committed to their wives' full human development, as women have been traditionally committed to supporting their husbands' development. This undoubtedly complicates family life quite a bit, especially when our institutions are still oriented to another plan. It might mean men diminishing their workload for a while so women can finish an advanced degree. It might mean negotiating the mobility of a family to maximize opportunities for both wife and husband.

Outcries will be heard that society will lose if men are not as exclusively devoted to their jobs. What is overlooked is that society will gain two skilled persons rather than one. We will have more wholistically developed men and women. We will have parenting that involves fathering as well as mothering. But the basic reason for the preference of partnership marriage over patriarchal marriage is justice. One person should not purchase fuller opportunities for human development at the expense of the diminishment of another.

If marriage is to be a just or fair covenant, it must be a covenant of mutuality—not advan-

tage on one side and disadvantage on the other; not submission on one side and dominance on the other.

It must be a covenant where mutual submission means mutual possibilities for human development for both partners to the contract.

Such a partnership marriage would change very much our conventional ideas of male and female plans of life. Instead of marriage meaning the end of female education and expansion and a sudden turn toward retirement into a restricted space, it would mean that men would have to modify their career pattern to enable women to maintain their education and development. But it would also mean that men would develop more diversified interests not tied to the job. They need not suffer the rapid decline and early death that often afflicts men in the retirement years.

Partnership marriage would also alter the images of maleness and femaleness. These stereotypes have not been based on "nature." They have been based on the hierarchical social relationships established between men and women by patriarchal society. As this pattern of relationship changes, the social traits of masculinity and femininity are revealed to a large extent as socially conditioned. Each half has been forced into a limited human development. Men have sometimes been allowed more androgyny (uniting of male and female traits) than women. As we have seen, the Christ-Church analogy for marriage allowed men to develop both "male" and "female" traits, while women were confined to one side of the relationship only. Partnership marriage recognizes the right of women to develop their capacities for articulateness, leadership and world shaping.

Most of all, partnership marriage means that the very relationship between the traits of nurturing, listening, and submitting, and those of leading and acting must be transformed. No longer can the relationship between these traits be modeled on dominant-submissive or exploitative relations. Listening and submitting will no longer be linked to powerlessness, nor acting and leading linked to domination. Rather, the ability to listen and give to others will be an expression of voluntary and free people. Our listening can be, in the true sense, gracious because no longer tacitly coerced. Our acting and leading will, in turn, be related to serving and nurturing the autonomy and development of one's partner, rather than using him or her for one's own ends. Mutuality transforms the very nature and quality of these relationships.

If patriarchal marriage ceases to provide a model for the covenant of Christ and the Church based on dominance-submission patterns, this might greatly change our image of the divine-human convenant also! Patriarchal marriage will no longer be there to foster an imagination about our relationship to Christ in terms of powerlessness and self-abnegation before an all-powerful authority figure. We can no longer be assured that all decisions will be taken care of for us by our "Lord."

Partnership marriage might also release quite different kinds of imagination about what relationship to God might mean. It means not only that we wait on God to act on our behalf, but also God waits on us to act on God's behalf! Relationship to God does not establish hierarchical relations between the human partners of the covenant, but rather establishes mutual relations. This might have something to do with Jesus' insistence that leadership in the Church is not modeled on dominance or mastery, but on service. The relationship to God might be seen as underlying and linking us to one another in relations of mutual service, not dominance and exploitation. Mutuality might be seen as the proper relationship not only between husband and wife, but between ministry and people, between political leaders and citizens, even between humanity and nature.

If it is true that without Christ we can do nothing, it is also said in the gospels that without the response of faith Christ can do no "mighty deeds." If we are called to be hearers of the Word, we are also called to be doers of it. Perhaps the delay of the Kingdom as the fulfillment of the Covenant has something to do with the fact that our models of relationship have inclined to hear too much of one side of the message and not enough of the other side. While we wait for God, God also waits for us to become responders to grace in building up—with and through God—the new heaven and earth.

9.

GOD'S NEW ISRAEL: AMERICA AS A COVENANTED NATION

The concept of the New Covenant, as it had been developed in early Christianity and was taken up by the Reformed and Anabaptist traditions, was first of all a religious bond. It was a relationship of salvation between God and humanity. Insofar as this covenant was the basis of a human community, this community was formed into a Church, a society of believers. Anabaptists particularly rejected any connections between this covenanted Church community and the state. However, for them too the covenant was seen as encompassing a total rule of life. It was not just a so-called religious dimension divorced from other secular activities in their lives. Thus the Church tended, for them too, to become a total community, embracing their social and economic life as well. This was particularly true in the separatist Anabaptist communities, such as the Hutterites. But their rejection of the sword and the magistracy made it impossible for these communities to coalesce with the state, in the sense of the government of nations.

It is in Calvinism, however, that we find the impulse to form covenanted Churches and also to use covenants as the basis of reformed political communities. Here we find the covenant spoken of not only in terms of salvation, but also as a new basis of nationhood. The covenant becomes the basis not only of ecclesiastical polity, but of a political polity founded on a national covenant. John Locke's concept of the Social Contract and the American concept of the Constitution have their roots in these Puritan theories of covenant-making.

The coextensiveness of religious and political community is found in Calvin's Geneva. Calvin's concept of the Christian commonwealth was that of a diarchy of ministry and magistracy. The ministry retained its independence to teach and propound the fundamentals of the biblical rule of faith and worship. The magistracy, as the political representatives of the people, had the power to consider, accept or reject these teachings. But once a consensus on the rules of common life had been reached between these two bodies, then the magistracy became the coercive arm of the Church. It punished moral infractions, such as cursing, drinking and stealing, and also religious infractions, such as heresy or even failing to come to church.

The entire community was to be shaped into a reformed and disciplined people. They should exhibit in their public lives what it means to be the commonwealth of Christ. The heretic might be burned and the truculently unregenerate expelled from the community. By purging the community of dissent and immorality, the political order itself might become "converted" and become a credible representative on earth of Christ's rule. It was still not the New Jerusalem, for the hidden dualism of elect and unelect still lay within it. The saints themselves were still forgiven sinners. But thus disciplined and purged, the political community could exhibit outwardly such reformed habits of life as to be a visible anticipation of Christ's rule and the theater of God's sovereignty on earth. In this way Calvinism moved in the direction of combining the religious and the political covenant.

These tendencies to interpret covenant politically were further developed in England, much influenced by Federal theology from Holland. Especially in the Scotch and English versions of Calvinism do we discover a claim to represent the New Israel as a covenanted nation. Through Puritan preaching in the sixteenth and seventeenth centuries, there is developed an idea of England as the New Israel covenanted with God as a special elect people. Here reappears the ancient Hebrew concept of covenant both as a religious bond with God and as the foundation of an elect nation.

However, many stricter Puritans were disappointed in these efforts. Moreover, the whole endeavor to create a reformed nation under a Puritan covenant was abandoned in England after twenty years of civil war and Cromwellian rule. Thus it was that the new colonies of America in the seventeenth century became the places where this Puritan dream of a covenanted commonwealth was developed. This intention to found a people under God, who have specifically contracted with God and with each other to be obedient to God's commandments of righteousness, is evident in the famous sermon of John Winthrop in 1630. Winthrop was first leader of the Massachusetts Bay colony and his sermon was delivered to the colonists while they were still on board ship:

> Thus stands the cause betweene God and us. Wee are entered into Covenant with him for this worke, wee have taken out a Commission, the Lord hath given us leave to draw our owne Articles, wee have professed to enterprise these Accions upon these and these ends, wee have hereupon besought him of favour and blessing. How if the Lord shall please to heare us, and bring us in peace to the place wee desire, then hath hee ratified this Covenant and sealed our Commission and will expect a strickt performance of the Articles contained in it, but if wee shall neglect the observacion of these Articles which are the ends wee have propounded and dissembling with our God, shall fall to embrace this present world and prosecute our carnall intencions seekeing greate things for our selves and our posterity, the Lord will surely breake out in wrathe against us, be revenged of such a perjured people and make us knowe the price of the breache of such a Covenant.

Winthrop goes on to say that the one way to avoid this shipwreck of their common purpose is to follow the teachings of the prophet Micah to "do justly and love mercy and walk humbly with our God" (6:8-AV). To this end the community must be "knit together as one man," hold each other in brotherly affection and be ready to "abridge ourselves of superfluities" in order to minister to each other in times of necessity. The community should rejoice together, mourn together, labor and suffer together, keeping before their eyes their common life as one Body in the Lord. If they do this, the Lord "will be our God and will delight to dwell amongst us as His own people and will command a blessing upon our ways."

Winthrop declares that the New England colony is to be like the city set on the hill. The eyes of all people are upon them, so that "if we deal falsely with our God in this work, and cause Him to withdraw his present help from us, we will become a shame to God's servants and cause them to turn their prayers to curses against us until we be consumed out of the good land where we are going." Winthrop ends his sermon with the Deuteronomic injunction of Moses in his last farewell to Israel before entrance to the Promised Land.

> Beloved there is now set before us life and good, death and evil in that we are commanded this day to Love the Lord our God and to love one another, to walk in his ways and keep his commandments and his ordinance and his laws, and the articles of our covenant with him that we may live and be multiplied and that the Lord our God may bless us in the land whither we go to the possess of it. But if our hearts shall turn away so that we will not obey, but shall be seduced and worship other gods, our pleasures and profits and serve them, it is pro-

> pounded unto us this day, we shall surely perish out of the good Land whither we pass over this vast sea to possess it.
>
> Therefore lett us choose life that wee and our Seede may live, by obeying his voyce and cleaveing to him, for hee is our life and our prosperity.[4]

In these passages we see how literally the New England colonists thought of themselves as a New Israel. They were renewing the covenant of Israel as an elect nation, rescued by God out of bondage and idolatry and brought into a Promised land. Land, peoplehood, and covenant are knit together in one theological vision of a renewed and righteous community elected by God to rebuild Zion in the wilderness of North America.

The covenant theology of the New England colonists had been the product of a complex development that brought together theological theories about the relationship between grace and works in divine-human relations, contract theories of government, and English national pride. Englishmen at this period were convinced that God had elected the English nation as champion of the Reformation against Roman Catholic Spain and France, to be the showcase of true faith and righteousness to the world.

Calvinism, with its strict doctrines of Divine predestination and human depravity, might not seem like a fruitful soil for ideas of human response to God in terms of voluntary contracts or commitments. The arguments over the extent of human free will and capacity to do "good works" raged in Dutch reformed thought. The Federal theologians developed an ingenious solution to this dilemma of divine election and human response. They distinguished between God's infinite will and nature and God's ordained will. God's infinite will and nature was mysterious and "past searching out." However, God has willed to make himself known to man by condescending to reveal himself in a set natural order and rule of morality. In so doing, God voluntarily limited himself in order to set up a finite order of nature and morality suited to man's limited nature. Thus God and man could enter into partnership on an equal basis.

But humanity has broken this original covenant of nature and has become irreparably indebted to God for its sins in a manner that could never be repaid. However, as a loving Father, God has further condescended, not only to human finiteness, but also to the fallen condition of humanity. God has renegotiated the original contract with humanity. He has agreed to make up himself, in Jesus Christ, the unpaid indebtedness of humankind for their broken contract. This the Puritans called the Covenant of Grace, anticipated already in the covenant with Abraham.

Now God no longer asks that humankind fulfill to the letter the whole moral law. God asks only that people respond in faith to this new covenant and agree to do their best to fulfill the moral law. The law of good works is still there, but it is no longer the basis of the contract. Rather it is the goal of continual striving. God's grace in repaying the earlier indebtedness is the basis of man's ability to enter this new covenant. It is God's own condescension to human limitations that made it possible for God and humanity to stand on an equal footing as contract partners.[5]

In this contract, humanity pledges itself with God to make the moral law and Christian faith (according to reformed standards) the basis of its life with each other and with him. In entering this contract the elect community pledges itself to strict self-discipline, not only individually but collectively. The moral law and reformed faith are to become the constitution of its community life. Its laws are to enact and uphold this norm and its magistrates to enforce it with all appropriate sanctions. Yet coercion of an unwilling people is eliminated as the basis of political life. The contract is not one which God forces upon the people, nor some people force upon others. Rather, according to the covenant ideal, it is a covenant which both God and humanity have entered willingly and voluntarily. Each member of the covenanted community likewise has consented to the covenant. Thus the mutual disciplines of the covenant become disciplines mutually accepted and agreed upon, founded not upon force, but upon the *consent of the governed.*

Such bonds are much more binding than those established by force, since all persons have consented to the mutual ties of government and taken upon themselves the common rules of the covenant as self-discipline. Thus each member of the covenant is responsible for the enforcement of the bonds of the covenant upon himself or herself, first of all, as well as fraternal admonishment of other members of the community. Because the contract is founded by common consent, infraction of it becomes much more heinous and culpable both in God's eyes and in those of other people. The saints pledge themselves to live up to a higher standard than that of the multitude of fallen humanity. Thereby they also accept a more severe standard of chastisement from God (and from their government) for their failings.

The Puritan extension of this concept of covenant to the political community drew upon and, in turn, became an important source for theories of constitutional government. The contract theory of government was a revolutionary idea in the seventeenth century. It was used to overthrow ideas of government based on natural or inherited hierarchy or divine right of kings. Feudal and royal ideas of government argued that the prince and his subjects were related to each other much as children were subject to their parents, or creatures subject to the paternal power of God.

Puritanism rejected the idea that any political leadership represented natural or divine fatherhood. Political leadership was a function within a community's agreement to form a society. No man inherited the right to rule by nature. Just as humanity contracted with God voluntarily to enter the covenant and to obey God's commands, so human government was based on a voluntary contract entered into willingly by all partners. In this contract humans pledged themselves to adhere to common disciplines of law and order and to receive thereby the blessings of peace and security.

It was the boldness of Puritan theory to try to bring together as one these theories of the covenant between humanity and God and the political contract of society. They postulated a Christian commonwealth founded upon the covenantal bond. In so doing, Puritan thought gave America a doublesided legacy. On the one hand it gave America a high consciousness of itself as an elect nation, specially favored by God, called to a higher mission than the rest of humanity, destined to prosper and succeed beyond all other nations because of this divine election and favor. On the other hand it exposed America to a higher level of criticism and judgement for any failures to live up to these high standards of covenanted life. Not for America the mistakes, pride, greed or naked power that the unregenerate nation might claim as the natural law of politics. Establishing itself as an elect nation under God, it must manifest a higher righteousness and be judged accordingly.

In the Puritan preaching of the seventeenth-century New England divines, we see this judgemental side of the concept of the covenant. God is said to have a Controversy with New England.[6] Like the prophets of the Old Testament, the New England Jeremiahs inveigh against their people for failing to live up to the strict terms of the covenant. God had rewarded their former piety with an abundance of material blessings. But now these same material blessings have allowed the people to grow fat and wanton and to neglect the terms of the covenant. Worldly manners have crept in among them. Standards of piety and frugality have become relaxed.

The ministers never openly imply that the people might become so unrighteous as to completely lose their covenanted relation to God. But they strongly hint that the covenanted relationship implies not only God's blessings upon obedient compliance, but also God's severe wrath and punishment upon its infraction. Moreover God is soon to bring his controversy with New England to a crisis. His patience is wearing thin. Only a short time remains for the people to repent and return to strict standards of life before some culminative act of divine vengeance will catch them. Natural catastrophes, droughts, floods, military defeats and raids from hostile French and Indians are all God's "medicines" of chastisement to bring the people to recognition of their laxity and return to full adherence to covenanted life.

Well into the eighteenth century, legislators as well as churchmen were exhorted to recognize that while a covenanted people enjoyed great privileges from God, this also entailed great duties and obligations.

> A covenant people are not left at their liberty, whether they will Love, Fear, Serve and Obey the voice of God in his Commands, or not. They are under the highest and most awful obligations imaginable to the whole of the Covenant duty; not only from God's express Command and Precept, who is their King, Lord and Lawgiver, but also, by virtue of their own Professed Subjection unto God . . . They are therefore most Solemnly cautioned to take heed to themselves and beware, lest they should forget and forsake the Lord, his Worship, Fear and Service, because by this means they would surely forfeit all those desirable blessings, which a course of obedience would crown them with, and pull down upon themselves the just rebukes and terrible revenges of Heaven.[7]

The ideas of America as a New Israel are the source of much that is good and bad in American history. On the one hand, the idea of America as an elect nation, specially blessed and favored, easily lends itself to extreme nationalism. On the other hand, those who take seriously the idea that covenant means a higher standard of righteousness take upon themselves the prophetic role in society. They castigate America for failures of justice, goodness, and righteousness, exhorting Americans again to rededicate themselves to the high standards of covenantal life. In our next chapter we will illustrate some of the ways the concept of America as an elect nation is read out as national arrogance and racist exclusivity, and also as prophetic self-criticism and national reform and renewal.

10.

THE EXPLOITATION OF THE COVENANT: THE ABUSES OF CHOSENNESS

The concept of a covenanted people in America may have entailed high ethical demands from the beginning. But the negative side of the concept of chosenness is the possibility of regarding the chosen ones as superior to others, more highly favored by God, with inherent rights over unchosen people. Who are the parties to the American social contract? For what purpose are they chosen? These are questions which returned to haunt Americans again and again as the nation absorbed more diversified populations and its role and power expanded in the world.

In 1776 the thirteen colonies revolted against the rule of English monarchy and contracted with each other to form a new government. Only a few of the New England states shared the Puritan concept of political life under God. They too had had to adjust their originally exclusive concepts of the Christian commonwealth to a more diversified and less disciplined reality. Other states, especially Virginia, were Anglican in foundation and thus represented religiously the Puritan Antichrist. Rationalist deism sat more easily with statesmen from this region than Calvinism. Yet leaders from these various colonies shared political ideas from the English and French Enlightenments propounded by thinkers such as John Locke and Baron Montesquieu. These thinkers had developed secular versions of the idea of the Social Contract.

Contract theories of government rejected the divine right of kings and inherited hierarchies. They believed in the formation of government through the consent of the governed. The establishment of a constitution as the basis of the American nation reflects this concept. Americans, in forming a new nation, were not merely rejecting dependence on England. They were rejecting one concept of government for another. They were declaring that the rules of law in a society are binding upon all only when all can be seen as voluntary parties to the social contract. The leaders and agents of social enforcement represent collective authority collectively assented to by all citizens.

But who really are the citizens? Who are the parties to the contract? The leaders of the colonists who assembled in Philadelphia were ready to apply the principle of the consent of the governed instead of monarchical rule from England over themselves. But were they willing to apply this same principle to many other persons in their midst who also had not been consulted about their government? What about the large percentage of persons who came to America, not voluntarily, but as bondservants? What about the servant and propertyless classes who had no voice in government? What about the Negro slaves, the most notable example of those who came to these shores involuntarily? Who consulted them about their government as they journeyed here in chains in fetid slave ships?

What about the American Indians whose lands were progressively taken over by the European immigrants? The colonies made treaties with the Indians for their land; they soon broke these treaties as westward expansion left less and less room for the Indian way of life. But no representatives of their peoples were invited to Philadelphia to sign the Constitution.

Finally, what about women? Are they a part of the citizen body? On what basis are all these people excluded from the Rights of Man so boldly proclaimed in the Declaration of Independence?

In 1776 Abigail Adams wrote her husband, John Adams, who was in Philadelphia attending the Continental Congress. Deliberately adopting the language of the American Revolution, she asked him to include women in the liberties which the Congress was seeking to safeguard:

> ...in the new code of laws which I suppose it will be necessary for you to make, I desire that you would remember the ladies and be more generous and favorable to them than your ancestors. Do not put such unlimited power into the hands of the husbands. Remember, all men would be tyrants if they could. If particular care and attention is not paid to the ladies, we are determined to foment a rebellion and will not hold ourselves bound by any laws in which we have no voice or representation.
>
> March 31, 1776[8]

In this letter Abigail Adams asserts the rights of women to be partners to the social contract. She rejects the paternalistic concept of fathers and husbands as the "natural representatives" of dependent persons. She warns against the certainty of tyranny whenever one person holds another in subjection.

John Adams' reply to this letter is instructive. The idea of including women in the consent of the governed he treats with humorous contempt. But, in the process, he inadvertently alludes to many other categories of persons who also were left unrecognized as partners to the social contract. While paternalism is rejected as a relationship between rulers and ruled for white, propertied males, paternalism is reasserted as the basis of social order for many other categories of persons whom he still regards as subjects to be governed by their masters. Only white propertied males are citizens and partners to the social contract. Women, Indians, slaves, servants and the propertyless are beneath or outside this contract, represented in it only indirectly through their masters. The feudal principle of natural hierarchy or paternalism is still the principle of government for these categories of persons.

> As to your extraordinary code of laws, I cannot but laugh. We have been told that our struggle has loosened the bonds of government everywhere; that children and apprentices were disobedient; that schools and colleges were grown turbulent; that Indians slighted their guardians and Negroes grew insolent to their masters. But your letter was the first intimation that another tribe, more numerous and more powerful than all the rest, were grown discontent. April 14, 1776[9]

The Civil War, the Indians Wars, the Civil Rights Movements, the Women's Movement were all to give the lie to these confident assertions. The concept of the consent of the governed as the basis of the American nation was too catching an idea to be confined to a small class of merchants and landowners. It implied, by its very nature, that the laws of the nation had no legitimacy for those who were excluded from citizenship. These struggles also showed a certain ability in the American principles of social covenant to expand to include more and more people in the consent of the governed. But this has not happened without tremendous pain, turmoil, bloodshed and vigorous campaigns of resistance on the part of those in power. In this struggle to expand the covenant, racial questions have loomed large.

Is there something intrinsically Protestant about the nature of American social institutions that makes it difficult to absorb Catholics? How Christian is the American Commonwealth? Can Jews be included? What about those whom Christians would have called "pagans"? If the covenant belongs to the "converted," how can it include those who don't share these Protestant or Christian principles of religion?

Furthermore, how Anglo-Saxon is the covenant? The English Puritans wove a close relationship between Protestantism and Anglo-Saxon or English peoplehood. God had made a special covenant with them to represent his favored people. The Puritans themselves escaped first to Holland and many learned their ideas from Geneva, so certain ecumenicity among Protestants of Northern European background was easily accepted. Yet the core of America was still seen as Anglo-Saxon in cultural identity. As more and more Irish Catholics, Italians, Poles, Jews from Eastern Europe, Greeks, Armenians and Asians poured onto these shores in successive waves of immigration, this latent ethnocentricity was to be strained to the breaking-point. The Anglo-Saxon racism that asserts itself throughout the nineteenth century against Blacks, Indians, Asians, Jews, and other so-called ethnics also surfaces these latent assumptions about the religious-racial exclusivity of the covenanting people of the United States.

Blacks have been the group most rigorously regarded as "beneath" the level of American peoplehood racially, although religiously they early adopted versions of evangelical Protestantism. A bloody Civil War was fought to abolish the institution of salvery—something the U.S. Constitution had failed to do. But many of the abolitionists had not yet come to terms with the idea of the equally *human nature* of Blacks and Whites. Even Abraham Lincoln, in his debates with Stephen Douglas in 1858, was not ready to accept this principle of human equality:

> I will say that I am not nor ever have been in favor of bringing about in any way the social and political equality of the white and black races . . . that I am not nor ever have been in favor of making voters or jurors of negroes, nor of qualifying them to hold office, nor to intermarry with white people, and I will say in addition to this that there is a physical difference between the white and black races which I believe will for ever forbid the two races living together on terms of social and political equality. And inasmuch as they cannot so live, while they do remain together there must be the position of superior and inferior, and I as much as any other man am in favor of having the superior position assigned to the white race.[10]

After a long destructive Civil War had torn the nation apart and largely destroyed the economy of the South, these words were to be legally negated. Congress voted in the Fourteenth Amendment to enfranchise the freedman. But the legal franchise did not guarantee its exercise in an America still no more ready than Lincoln had been in 1858 to recognize a common humanity shared by Blacks and Whites alike. The Jim Crow laws, passed in one after another Southern state in the 1880s, effectively removed the franchise that had been granted by this amendment. Black men and women were reduced to a status of socially segregated inferiority. It was not until the 1960s that Americans again took up the struggle against these laws of segregation. Blacks still remain today the single greatest challenge to the American acceptance of racial pluralism within the one nation.

The implicit whiteness or Anglo-Saxonism of American nationhood was expressed in reactions to many other groups. Americans have been fond of speaking of their nation as a melting-pot. But the melting-pot from the beginning had a certain mold marked White-Anglo-Saxon-Protestant. Some groups melted into this mold much more easily than others. The American Indian has been the second great casualty of American racism. Their history has been quite distinct from Blacks. Blacks were people stolen from their own land and tribal nationhood and brought to these shores to work as exploited labor. They have experienced a rejection of their full humanity and a refusal to allow them to integrate as full citizens. Indians, on the other hand, held the land the colonists wanted.

From the very beginning of the colonial settlement, Indians were regarded as the opposite of the Puritan view of converted or redeemed humanity. In their eyes the Indian was the savage, the natural or fallen human. They were unregenerate and, many Puritans soon became convinced, unredeemable. Their fate was marked out as one of physical or cultural extermination. The more kindly view of this process, expounded especially by missionaries, was the conversion of the Indians. They were subjected to a more or less forced integration into American society; Indians were supposed to disappear as a distinct people. The more unkindly view, acted out in the long Indian Wars, was to see them as no more than a pestilent animal population to be wiped out by advancing "civilization."

Reservations segregated them in the least arable lands. But even these treaties were soon violated as new wealth was found on these lands. The basic predicament of Indians is that Americans have never really accepted their right to survive as autonomous nations with a distinct culture and land base. The American Indian Movement of the 1960s and 70s had tried to reassert once more the independent peoplehood of the Indians. But the destruction of this people is already so advanced that it is not clear whether any better outcome can be salvaged from this sorry history.

In 1855 Oliver Wendell Holmes expressed in elegant tones the general American assumption that the Indian is a people marked out for extermination by the "higher" and more favored white race.

> Theologians stand aghast at a whole race destined, according to their old formulae, to destruction, temporal and eternal. Philanthropists

> mourn over them and from time to time catch a red man and turn him into their colleges as they would turn a partridge in among the barn-door fowls. But instinct has its way sooner or later; the partridge makes but a troublesome chicken and the Indian but a sorry Master of Arts, if he does not run for the woods, where all the *ferae naturae* impulses are urging him. These instincts lead to his extermination; too often the sad solution of the problem of his relation to the white man . . . . Then the white man hates him, and hunts him down like the wild beasts of the forest, and so the red-crayon sketch is rubbed out, and the canvas is ready for a picture of manhood a little more like God's own image.[11]

In this statement Holmes represents the popular nineteenth-century restatement of the Puritan doctrine of the WASP's divinely-favored place in history. English Puritans had believed that God had elected the English people to be the demonstration of reformed religion and morality. Americans of the second half of the nineteenth century were restating these ideas of divine election in terms of racial biology and evolution. The success of the white race, both in conquering the American continent and spreading its power through the world, was seen as proof positive of its racial superiority.

Natural selection thus replaces God as the force of predestination. Survival of the fittest proves that those who win are the best. Viewing the world through this lens of social Darwinism, Americans looked with complacency upon their own extermination of Indians, conquest of Mexicans in the Southwest, and expansion into the Pacific sphere. Like their British forebears to whose Empire they believed they were destined to succeed, Americans thought their very success was proof of their right to lead and conquer the other peoples of the world.

But this confident vision of Anglo-Saxon American Manifest Destiny was more than a little disturbed by the increasing racial and religious pluralism that began to characterize the nation in the later nineteenth century. The potato famine brought wave upon wave of immigrants from Ireland. The pogroms of Russia filled New York and other cities with Jewish refugees. Rapid industrialization was shaping huge urban ghettos of tenements and sweatshops. Much of this new factory labor was not being furnished by people of the old racial stocks. What would happen to Anglo-Saxon manifest destiny if the Elect Nation itself came to have only a minority of Anglo-Saxons and Protestants? White Americans responded to the immigration crisis in two ways: with an increasing cry to limit immigration of non-white populations, and with efforts to keep disenfranchised and socially inferior those people not yet "Anglo-Saxonized."

Orientals, especially Chinese, began to immigrate to the western side of the continent with the Gold Rush and the building of the continental railroads. They were the first people treated to an explicitly racial ban on immigration. In 1865 an editorial in the *New York Times* expressed this view of racial bars to immigration:

> Now we are utterly opposed to the permission of an extensive emigration of Chinamen or other Asiatics to any part of the United States. There are other points of national well-being to be considered beside the sudden development of material wealth. The security of its free institutions is more important. . . . The maintenance of an elevated national character is of higher value than mere growth in physical power. . . . With Oriental blood will necessarily come Oriental thoughts and the attempt at Oriental social habits. . . .
>
> We already have four millions of degraded negroes in the South . . . and if there were to be a floodtide of Chinese population—a population befouled with all the social vices, with no knowledge or appreciation of free institutions or constitutional liberty, with heathenish souls and heathenish propensities, whose character and habits and modes of thought are firmly fixed by the consolidating influence of ages upon ages—we should be prepared to bid farewell to republicanism and democracy.[12]

In the 1880s and 90s the Immigration Restriction League campaigned for legislation against so-called non-Aryan settlement. John Burgess, professor at Columbia University, expressed the League's view that the very nature of the American commonwealth, its political institutions and cultural consensus, demanded such exclusion:

> What folly, on the part of the ignorant, what wickedness on the part of the intelligent, are involved in the attempts . . . to pollute the United States with non-Aryan elements . . . . We must preserve our Aryan nationality in the state, and admit to its membership only such non-Aryan race-elements as shall have become Aryanized in spirit and in genius by contact with it, if we would build the superstructure of the ideal American commonwealth.[13]

Are there limits to becoming Aryanized in spirit? Can a German do it, but not a Pole, an Irishman or an Italian? Can Jews become Aryan in spirit? Are some races—Black, Orientals, Indians—excluded by their very biology from this capacity? These questions are left unanswered by Burgess. What is denied is the possibility that the social covenant of American society itself might be renegotiated. How might cultural groups that were not a party to the original contract contribute more than just their minds and bodies to be assimilated? How might they preserve their own distinct cultures and histories in order to add them to the mix?

Becoming an American would then mean learning not just Puritan history of Massachusetts, but Black history and Indian histories as the other side of this Anglo-Saxon history. How might the heroic tale of Scandinavian settlement in Minnesota, Jewish flight from Russia to America, Chicano struggle in the Southwest, and many others also become memories and heritages that all Americans can learn as a part of their national identity? The story of *Hester Street;* of *The Emigrants;* the book and televised versions of *Roots*; the popular best-seller, *Bury My Heart at Wounded Knee*: all these represent belated attempts by Americans to learn these suppressed histories.

11.

THE CRITIQUE OF THE COVENANT: THE SOCIAL CONTRACT BROKEN AND RENEWED

The idea of America as an elect nation implied divine favor and blessing, but this was conditional upon obedience to God's commands of righteousness. Thus the concept of the covenant also can imply social criticism. The statements about human rights, equality, and justice in the Declaration of Independence are read as a mandate of high ethical demands, equally applicable to all persons in the American community. To fail to seek justice and equality for all is to betray the covenant upon which America is founded. Reverses of fortune and social turmoil are divine chastisements for these failures. Thereby God intends to bring American leaders to repentance and to a renewed effort to fulfill the ideals of the covenant.

However, the covenantal nature of American society can be read in two ways. On the one hand, the covenant can be read as giving a status of favor to America that is already assured. Divine favor is a possession America has by its very nature. It confers a superiority that justifies triumphalistic attitudes toward other less-favored persons.

A second way of reading the covenantal relation of God and America is to see this as commandment rather than favor. God demands justice from his people and thus punishes them more severely when they fail to live up to a high standard of social ethics. In this reading, favor and blessing are not possessions, but a future aspiration conditional upon continued striving after the divine standard of social righteousness. Precisely because God loves this people more than the others, he is a more exacting judge of their failings. The covenant is not a static framework for self-glorification, but rather the impulse for continual revolutionary renewal. The covenant unfolds continually, disclosing a fuller vision of what social justice means.

It is not sufficient to see the rights of citizenship for Whites and not for Blacks, for men and not for women. Civil justice implies economic justice. Implications of the covenant left unrecognized by the founding fathers become starkly evident to a later generation—and in this way the covenant becomes prophetic and futuristic. Its commandments go ahead of the community, judging their failures and urging them on to new efforts to repent of these failings and to build anew the ideal commonwealth. This prophetic interpretation is far more authentic to the biblical understanding of the covenant.

In American history there have been continual waves of revolutionary renewal seeking to reform the basis of the American social contract and set before it a fuller ideal of social justice. These waves of intense self-criticism and demand for fundamental reforms are not accidental to American life. They are deeply rooted in the biblical foundations of the idea of election and covenant. We will mention four important examples of such reform movements: Abolitionism; Women's Rights; the Social Gospel; and the Civil Rights Movement.

The most outstanding contradiction to the stated ideals of universal human rights in the Declaration of Independence was the subsequent condoning of slavery in the American Constitution. Christian conscience had been slow to confront the slavery question ethically. The early Church fathers had allowed themselves to accept the institution of slavery by spiritualizing the emancipation brought by Christ. Since Christ freed us spiritually, the fact that our bodies were in slavery was regarded as unimportant. Slavery was also seen as a part of the unfortunate, but necessary, order of nature as adapted by God to the reality of sin. On these grounds, the Christian churches did not seriously protest against slavery or regard it as sinful for Christians to hold slaves. Only toward the end of the eighteenth century did some Christians on the radical fringes of the Church, especially Quakers, begin to condemn slavery as fundamentally sinful.

Many of the founding fathers were deeply disturbed by slavery. They felt it was wrong for one man to hold another in bondage. But they were more concerned that the slavery issue would split the North from the South and make it impossible to form a Union. They were further influenced by their views of the sacred nature of property rights. Most fundamentally, few Whites could really imagine living with Blacks as equals, so convinced were they that Blacks by their very nature were inferior and alien. Because those who had misgivings about slavery capitulated, the convention in Philadelphia passed a Constitution that legitimated slavery in the Southern states.

In the 1830s the protests against slavery began to rise into an organized movement. Some leaders, like William Lloyd Garrison, felt that the Constitution itself was invalid because it condoned this most intolerable injustice. He condemned the Constitution uncompromisingly as "a covenant with Death and an agreement with Hell." A Union so constituted had been covenanted with Satan, not with God. No statement could have more sweepingly disavowed the Puritan view that the American state was founded as a nation under God. Yet in Garrison's very condemnation is a righteous anger that is also rooted in these same Puritan assumptions. A covenant with God demands a recognition that all are free, all citizens, all children of God. Anything that fundamentally contradicts that is not a covenant with God, but with his adversary.

The great Negro abolitionist Frederick Douglass once declared that it is impossible for anyone to take an oath to uphold the Constitution. To take such an oath implies that the Constitution embodies a consistent set of principles. But, in fact, it contradicts itself by speaking of life, liberty and the pursuit of happiness as the natural rights of "all men," while denying these rights to Black slaves. The Constitution thus presented demands that we serve two masters. No one could uphold both these views at the same time.[14]

Other abolitionists took a less drastic view. Theodore Weld felt that the basic principles of the American creed were valid, but they had not been consistently applied. The Constitution need not be rejected, but rather it should be reformed, using its fundamental principles to eradicate the inconsistency of slavery. In 1861 the Southern states fulfilled the fears of the founding fathers. By seceding from the Union they, too, declared that the Union thus formed, half-slave and half-free, could not endure. If the principles of freedom became normative for all, then the Southern slave states would have to leave the Union. Only the Civil War, which abolished slavery in the South and kept the Confederate states in the Union by force, settled the issue in practice, if not in theory. The covenant was reformed and set on a new basis by enormous bloodletting. But the scars have yet to heal fully in the American body politic.

In the abolitionist period, that rebellion of women with which Abigail Adams threatened her husband in 1776 began to make itself felt also. Most of the early feminists, such as Sarah and Angelina Grimké, Elizabeth Cady Stanton, Lucretia Mott and Susan B. Anthony, began their political life in abolitionism. But when they were frequently denied the rights to act and speak on behalf of the slave because they were women —when they found it necessary to form Female Anti-Slavery Societies— they began to realize that they had to organize in behalf of another great disenfranchised minority as well.

In the Civil War period women not only were denied the vote, they were defined legally as lifetime minors—dependent on father or husband, having no legal rights to represent themselves, hold property, make contracts, or in other ways act as legal adults. Women also were denied higher education and access to employment and professions. The Women's Movement, which gradually altered this historic status of women, was a prolonged struggle that went on from the 1840s until the vote was finally won in 1920. Even today many remnants of the inferior legal and economic status of women remain.

In 1848 two leading feminists, Elizabeth Cady Stanton and Susan B. Anthony, assembled the first Women's Rights convention in Seneca Falls, New York. Like the radical abolitionists, they declared that the American Social Contract was fundamentally deficient because it failed to recognize women as equal citizens. Until that defect was remedied, women must regard the American covenant as in fundamental violation of the laws of nature and nature's God in whose name the covenant purports to be founded. Consciously modeling their Declaration of Women's Rights on the American Declaration of Independence, the women declared:

> We hold these truths to be self-evident: that all men and women are created equal; that they are endowed by their creator with certain inalienable rights . . . .
> When a long train of abuses and usurpations, pursuing invariably the same object evinces a design to reduce them under absolute despotism, it is their duty to throw off such government and to provide new guards for their future security. Such has been the patient sufferance of women under this government, and such is now the necessity which constrains them to demand the equal station to which they are entitled.

The women then detail the list of these "abuses and usurpations":

1. Withholding the franchise.
2. Non-representation in the laws to which she is called to submit.
3. Denial of basic civil rights.
4. The status of "civil death" of the married woman.
5. Withholding of property rights, even to her own wages.
6. The subjugation to a state of servitude to her husband, even to the extent of giving him the right of corporal punishment.
7. Neglect of female interests and rights of children in divorce laws.
8. Taxation without representation.
9. Withholding of profitable employment and giving of unjust wages in those jobs which women are allowed to pursue.

10. Denial of higher education.
11. The subordinate position of women in the Church, including the denial of the ministry.
12. The double standard in sexual morality.
13. The usurpation by men of the role of God as lawgiver in the giving of unjust laws, sanctified by religion.
14. The promotion of a culture and social conditioning designed to lessen in every way women's self-confidence in her own powers and to make her dependent on men.

The women sum up their views by saying:

> In view of this entire disenfranchisement of one half of this country, their social and religious degradation–in view of the unjust laws above mentioned, and because women do feel themselves aggrieved, oppressed and fraudulently deprived of their most sacred rights, we insist that they have immediate admission to all the rights and privileges which belong to them as citizens of the United States.[15]

Once more the social contract of American society is declared invalidated because it fails to live up to the fuller understanding of justice. But once again a group not recognized as among the original covenant partners claims the rights and privileges of that contract. They evoke its own principles to judge it and demand its reform.

The acceptance of this demand was to come slowly and often piecemeal. But gradually the redefinition of the American Constitution called for at Seneca Falls was accepted. The principles of the covenant proved capable of reforming its earlier defects. The very universalism of its declaration of natural rights was an expansive thesis, opening it up to more and more categories of people previously excluded.

The third great reform movement of American society can be described as the Social Gospel. It occurred mainly between 1880 and 1920, although many of the demands for labor reform were not effected until the Roosevelt administrations of the 1930s. The Social Gospel movement deepened the American sensitivity to social justice. Civil liberties are not enough without economic justice.

In the 1880s America was a nation that was changing rapidly from the country of farms and small towns to an industrialized nation of great cities. Wealth increased rapidly. Between 1860 and 1890 the national wealth increased by 600%, but over half this wealth was held by .03% of the population. There were great extremes of wealth and poverty. On the one end of the scale the fabulous wealth of the Vanderbilts and Rockefellers was being founded. On the other end were the teeming slums and sweatshops where immigrant labor toiled long hours for miserable wages. This was the period in which America was being peopled by waves of new immigrants with ethnic backgrounds different from the original settlers. There was a fear that the old Anglo-Saxon America would lose its national identity. At the same time, the rising racism of the era helped condone brutal and exploitative working conditions for these newer groups.

However, not all Americans responded with racist and self-justifying tones to this situation of growing injustice. Some Americans took it as a challenge to reform our economic system. The very nature of democracy, these critics felt, meant that it must be extended from the civil-libertarian to the economic spheres. The new industrial worker must become a co-owner and co-manager of the factory where he (or she) worked. Only if democratic principles were applied to the economic realm could the interests of the workers be safeguarded.

Liberal Protestant churchmen took the lead in formulating this economic critique of American society. Untrammeled competition and the right of the stronger were no part of authentic Christianity, they argued. The essence of Christianity was community, love and "brotherhood." All members of the Christian community were members of one body. In social terms, this meant an ethic of socialization of the means of production, profit-sharing, and assurance of a just wage for all workers. Ruthless competition and the pursuit of self-interest in disregard for the neighbor were condemned in Christianity as sinful selfishness. The socialist hope for a future society of mutuality and justice was seen as harmonizing with the Christian hope for the Kingdom of God.

This does not mean that the churchmen thought that the socialist goal was equivalent to the Christian hope for Christ's Kingdom. However, there was a correspondence between the socialist goal and the Christian ideal. The Christian ideal was deeper and higher, but encompassed the socialist goal within its vision of what a redeemed humanity on a redeemed earth should mean. When socialists attacked the exploitation of the worker, this was in line with the prophetic attack on the exploitation of the poor by the rich. Socialist hopes for a cooperative social order were in keeping with Christian doctrines of fellowship and community. The future hopes for a new socialist order were in the same direction as the Christian expectation of a new heaven and earth of reconciliation and peace—except that Christian hope demanded a deeper regeneration of the human nature. It was along these lines that advocates of the Social Gospel in the late nineteenth and early twentieth centuries lined up Christianity, the American dream of equality and justice, and the socialist critique of economic injustice.

Many Americans persisted in seeing socialism as un-American, not to say un-Christian. Human rights and demands for justice stopped at the level of equality before the law. They did not include economic rights. But gradually many Americans began to realize that social community involved a certain economic responsibility for all the citizens. The corporate wealth of a nation was not just "private property." It was a national wealth that demanded a certain distribution among all the citizens, at least on the level of basic needs for food, shelter and education. Nor could the so-called law of the market justify making people work as long as possible, for as little as possible, under the most dangerous conditions. Industry must accept minimum wages, limited work hours, and basic standards of protection of life and health.

In 1908 the Methodist Episcopal Church adopted the following social creed at their General Conference in Baltimore. It represents the basic principles of the Social Gospel accepted by liberal churchmen of the period:

> The Methodist Episcopal Church stands:
> For equal rights and complete justice for all men in all stations of life.
> For the principle of conciliation and arbitration in industrial dissensions.
> For the protection of the worker from dangerous machinery, occupational diseases, injury and mortality.
> For the abolition of child labor.
> For such regulation of the conditions of labor for women as shall safeguard the physical and moral health of the community.
> For the suppression of the "sweating system."
> For the gradual and reasonable reduction of the hours of labor to the lowest practical point, with work for all, and for that degree of leisure for all which is the condition of the highest human life.
> For a release from employment one day in seven.
> For a living wage in every industry.
> For the highest wage that each industry can afford and for the most equitable division of the products of industry that can ultimately be devised.
> For the recognition of the Golden Rule and the mind of Christ as the supreme law of society and the sure remedy of all social ills.[16]

Some of these demands were met in subsequent social legislation. Many of them remain utopian even today. Americans still face rising unemployment and a national distribution of wealth that leaves one family in eight below the poverty line, while a tiny minority possess the lion's share. Economic questions that the Christian socialists were considering two generations ago continue to be relevant. To what extent must a Christian ethic be an ethic of economic justice? To what extent does the American creed—which guarantees to all persons the basic means of human development–have to take into consideration a critique of an economic system that leaves many without fulfillment of basic needs? In the future, the challenges to the Christian conscience in an American context may well put the ethics of economic justice at the center of the stage.

After the Civil War, the enslaved Negro was freed and given the rights of citizenship. But having accomplished this, the American conscience shows an alarming desire to put the "colored question" on the back burner. "Binding up the wounds of the nation" came to mean, all too often, looking the other way while state after state passed laws relegating Blacks to an inferior legal caste. The N.A.A.C.P. was founded at the turn of the century to fight these Jim Crow laws. But it was not until the late 1950s that this struggle erupted into the center of the American social conscience. Led by the dynamic Martin Luther King, Jr., Americans of all religions and social backgrounds marched together in the fight for Civil Rights, to win back the rights that had been stolen from Blacks in the 1880s.

Martin Luther King, Jr., might well be credited with being America's greatest orator of civil religion. It was he who most clearly grasped the biblical prophetic roots of the American blend of social contract and religious covenant. King translated this language of the American creed from a language of self-sanctification back into the biblical challenge to build the beloved community: to do justice and love mercy and walk humbly with our God.

King made the American language of civil rights again echo with the accents of Amos, Micah, Jeremiah and the other prophets. When he cried "Let justice roll down like waters and righteousness like an ever-flowing stream," we felt the mighty hand of the Just God about to strike the sinful nation. When he called to us to let "every valley be lifted up, every mountain and hill be made low, the uneven ground smooth, that the glory of the Lord shall be revealed and all flesh shall see it together," we felt the momentous stirrings of the biblical ideal of the redeemed community. This was not a remote dream, but a command laid upon this nation at this time. In pulling down the unjust racist laws and exalting those who had been humiliated–in teaching all Americans, Black and White, to walk "hand in hand together"–we were beginning the fulfillment of this ancient hope. Here: in the red hills of Georgia; in the blood-stained fields of Mississippi; perhaps even in the hate-filled streets of Cicero and South Boston. Martin Luther King, Jr., stirred again the biblical roots of the American social compact and made us see it anew as a pact between humanity and God to build a better world.

Then all too quickly that stirring of excitement faded into new apathy and alienation. It seemed as though problems overwhelmed us in their multitude and complexity. To build the beloved community by integrating a lunch counter seemed do-able. But when the arena of conflict shifted from the small world of the Southern town to the institutionalized racism of the Northern city–when we began to see racism as a structure of poverty endemic to our social and economic system, keeping Blacks at the bottom in America–when we saw the same structure of racism exploiting poor people, mostly of colored hue, in many nations, backed up by a formidable system of international corporations and international militarism–the tasks of justice seemed to escape our capacities. It seemed easier to turn inward again to find methods of self-realization; easier to pursue our small worlds of survival and success. We could not worry our heads about grand visions of redeeming our society, not to mention the world as a whole.

"Are we still serviceable?" The question that Bonhoeffer asked himself and his community in Germany in the 1940s might well be the question American Christians ask themselves today. The American union of covenant and social contract has been the source of much that is the best, and much that is the worst in us. It has been the source of exploitative selfishness and triumphalism. But, again and again, it has been rediscovered as prophetic self-criticism and the call to renewed dedication to build the just society.

Today we await a new burst of that God-given energy and grace to tackle the great questions of our day: economic injustice, lingering racism, sexism, rampant militarism and patterns of consumerism that pollute the earth and threaten the very foundations of human life on earth. In the words of Moses in Deuteronomy, quoted by the Puritan founder John Winthrop, and again by the new President Jimmy Carter in his inaugural address:

> I have set before you this day life and death, blessing and curse; thereforce choose life, that you and your descendants may live. (Deut. 30:19)

12.

THE EVALUATION OF THE COVENANT

We have seen that the concept of the covenant is a guiding theme in Scripture, both Old and New Testament, and in much of Christian history. Needless to say, in Judaism as well, the concept of the covenant remains central. The rabbinic tradition continues to maintain that the Jewish people are an elect nation, called by God into a specially covenanted relationship. This relationship to God entails the responsibilities of obedience to the Torah and witnessing to the one God and the moral law to the other nations. Through obedience to the Torah, the messianic age will be brought near.

The history of covenantal relationship to God in Judaism, in the Christian Church, and in American history, which we have discussed in these chapters, raises many questions. The various uses of the idea of covenant are not easily reconciled with each other. How exclusive is the covenant? Or, how universal is it? Is there one covenant or many? Can it be reformed and renewed? Can it be broken so irrevocably that it is transferred to another people? Are its duties and responsibilities secular or spiritual? Are its promises of future blessings this-worldly or otherworldly? All of these different views have been espoused within the Jewish and Christian traditions at one time or another.

One important area of controversy for covenantal theology is Jewish-Christian relations. Christianity maintains that it is the people of the New Covenant. This New Covenant is in fulfillment of the promises of Jeremiah:

> Behold, the days are coming, says the Lord, when I will make a new covenant with the house of Israel and the house of Judah, not like the

> covenant which I made with their fathers when I took them by the hand to lead them out of the land of Egypt, my covenant which they broke. . . . This is the covenant which I will make with the house of Israel after those days, says the Lord: I will put my law within them, and I will write it upon their hearts . . . for I will forgive their iniquity, and I will remember their sin no more. (Jer. 31:31-34)

This new covenant is thought of as more internalized than the old covenant. The old covenant was one which people had to teach each other; the new covenant is written on people's hearts. It has become, so to speak, their new spiritual nature. In Christian language it is no longer law, but grace; no longer letter, but spirit. This new covenant is associated in prophecy with the fulfillment of a messianic future. The Christian Church claims that that messianic future has already been revealed in Jesus Christ. Through his death and resurrection, the power of baptism in the Holy Spirit has already been made available. In the words of Paul:

> Our sufficiency is from God, who has qualified us to be ministers of a new covenant, not in a written code but in the Spirit; for the written code kills, but the Spirit gives life. (2 Cor. 3:5-6)

The new covenant of spiritual obedience is thought of as an eschatological possibility—a possibility that is fulfilled only in the final future Reign of God. And yet because its first fruits have already been made available in Jesus the Christ, it also comes to be seen in Christianity as a historical possibility. It is a new dispensation within history that founds a new people, the Christian people. This new people inherits the covenant of Israel, superseding and fulfilling the old covenant. The old commandments of the Torah are no longer in force, at least as concerns ritual law. Even as regards moral law, the Christian dispensation is believed to make available a "better righteousness" based on faith and grace—no longer on good works. Moreover this new people, the Church, is a universal people—no longer a particular people. Theirs is a covenant that dissolves the distinction of Jew and Greek. It is open to all nations. In Christ there is neither Jew nor Greek, slave nor free, male nor female (Galatians 3:28).

Yet these claims of Christianity to be the New Israel of the new covenant raise many problems. Is it fair to speak of Jewish law as "mere letter"? This dualism of law and grace is quite foreign to Judaism. For them, too, the law is a gift. The commandment of good works is not possible without the prior blessings of the gift of election and Torah. There is imperfection in obedience and the constant need for forgiveness. Neither are Christians absolved from good works, but must make a new beginning based on forgiveness of sins. It seems that the letter (or good works) has not been superseded in Christianity. Rather, the dialectic between grace and good works, letter and spirit, is restated in a new way.

Moreover, is it correct to say that the eschatological promises have *already* been fulfilled? Is it not that we have a *foretaste* of this blessing in Jesus? But that final conquest of evil, when every tear is wiped away and all evil ceases, is as much ahead of the Christian people as it is of the Jewish people. We too struggle in an imperfect world and await a future fulfillment of our hope in return of Christ on clouds of glory. Perhaps Christians should not think of themselves as inheriting the covenant from Israel in the sense of *superseding* the old Israel and leaving it behind in a state of reprobation until Jews convert to our new covenant. Rather perhaps we should see that, historically, what has happened is that the religion of the Old Testament gave birth in the first centuries of the common era to two paths: Christianity and Rabbinic Judaism. Each thinks of itself as a covenanted people–Christians as completing the old covenant and anticipating the messianic covenant; Judaism as continuing and giving further explication, through the rabbinic commentaries, to the commands of the covenant of Sinai. Each appropriates the past covenant in a different way. Each goes forward on the basis of experiences of grace and mandates of action in a still sinful world, awaiting the final "solution to the riddle of history"[17] which is still to come.

Such rethinking of the relations between Judaism and Christianity raises difficulties n both sides. Judaism does not accept the idea that there has been a second covenant given to the Christian people–a people who are Gentile, who do not keep the Torah, the commandments of the covenant. Christians, in turn, do not readily accept the idea that Judaism is a parallel rather than a superseded faith. They hesitate to say that Judaism has a path to salvation, independent of Jesus Christ, and still based on the covenant of Sinai.

There have been various attempts to mediate this dispute between Jews and Christians over the inheritance of the covenant. One important such dialogue took place between the Jew, Rosenstock-Huessy, and the converted Jew, Franz Rosenzweig. Rosenzweig's reasoning is relevant to us, for he argued that Judaism and Christianity should be considered related to each other as a fire is related to its rays. Judaism is still the center of God's election, through which the central messages of monotheism and ethical life are transmitted. Christianity is the expression of the mission of Israel to the Gentiles. Through the Church this message of Israel is transmitted to the world. Christianity is the universalization of Israel for the sake of all nations. A Christian theologian, Paul van Buren, has recently adopted this same paradigm for the relationship of Judaism and Christianity.[18]

Such a concept of the relationship of the Jewish and Christian dispensations has much to recommend it, but it doesn't quite do justice to the reality of either group or their distinctive views of their identities. It makes Judaism sound too limited to a particular people, in a racial or ethnic sense. In fact, Judaism, widespread as a faith and a community, has gathered people from many nations. The ethnic pluralism of that people called Jews is evident to any visitor to Israel. On the other side, Christianity has taken on elements of particularism and has become identified with particular peoples. In the English and American traditions especially, the idea of the Christian covenant has become identified with the national identities of particular peoples; it has been used to chart and judge their national destinies.

Thus covenantal theology remains an important unresolved area of Jewish-Christian relations. It has not been easy for Jews and Christians to engage in dialogue at all. This is because Christians have generally assumed that there could only be one authentic end of the dialogue—Jewish conversion to Christianity. All else was hardness of heart on the part of Jews. Jews have regarded this conclusion as totally unacceptable, tantamount to the annihilation of Judaism. Today, in a more open ecumenical relation that has developed between the two faiths, especially in the United States, a new dialogue might be mutually fruitful. This would be a dialogue based on the assumption that each faith would recognize the integrity of the other. There may be no better place to start such dialogue than on the topic of covenantal theology.

Many problems still arise concerning covenantal theology in the Christian tradition. The early Christian Church spiritualized the concept of the Promised Land. This land and the future age of blessedness were not referring to a particular land on earth or a future historical age to come. Rather, according to these early Christians, the promised land is heaven. The future age is an eternal age that will come when this present finite earth is swallowed up. The messianic future is other-worldly, not this-worldly. It refers to life after death—not to a future historical era. Most Christians continue to follow this other-worldly understanding of the Kingdom of God.

However, even within the New Testament and the early Christian theologians, two ideas of the messianic future appear side by side. The second idea suggests that there will be a future historic age of blessedness occurring on earth as the thousand-year reign of Christ. Only after this period will the old heaven and earth be destroyed and a new eternal heaven and earth appear (Revelation 20-21). Groups of Christians down through history have continued to follow or revive this idea of a historical millennium.

In the modern era we find many social philosophies and theologies which revive the idea of a secular messianic age. Liberal theologies, as expressed by philosophers such as Emmanuel Kant and theologians such as Albrecht Ritschl, theologies of Social Gospel or Christian Socialism—even anti-religious social philosophies such as Marxism—are based on an idea of history that must be fulfilled through a final culminative age of goodness, peace and justice on earth. Whether this good age be brought about through evolution or through revolution, much of the social philosophy that continues to inspire modern groups in the West and, especially today, in Asia, Africa and Latin America, is based on secular versions of messianic hope. The messianic promises must be fulfilled on earth, not in heaven. They are a moral and political task of humanity; not an eschatological intervention from heaven. Emmanuel Kant speaks of this historic fulfillment of human destiny on earth in accents that sound this theme in modern thought:

> We have good reason to say that the Kingdom of God has come upon us once the principle of the gradual transition of ecclesiastical faith to the universal religion of reason and so to a (divine) ethical state on earth has become general and has gained somewhere a public foothold, even though the actual establishment of this state is still infinitely removed from us. For since this principle contains the basis for a continual approach toward such a consummation, there lies in it invisibly as a seed which is self-developing and self-fertilizing, the whole which is one day to illuminate and rule the world. But truth and goodness . . . do not fail to communicate themselves far and wide . . . erecting for itself in the human race regarded as a commonwealth under the laws of virtue, a power and a kingdom which sustains the victory over evil and, under its own dominion, assures the world of eternal peace.[19]

Another important aspect of differing views of the Christian covenant has to do with relations between Church and state. In Judaism the covenant founded both a religious community and a nation. The two indeed were one people. The Davidic kings, the rulers of Israel politically, also belonged within the covenant and were bound by its obedience. There was no separation of Church and state. The laws of the covenant ruled not only a "religious dimension" of peoples' lives, but ruled the whole of peoples' lives legally and morally. The Jewish courts administered the laws of the Torah as the legal code of the Jewish community.

However in A.D. 70, with the fall of Jerusalem in the Jewish wars against the Roman empire, the Jews ceased to occupy their historical homeland as the base of national identity. After this time, Jews had to survive as a scattered people among many nations. The Torah continued to be the internal law of the Jewish community, but externally they were ruled by the laws of other states. It is only in recent years that a Jewish state has again been founded.

Christianity, from its early beginnings, separated itself as a religious community from ethnic Israel and concepts of a Jewish state. For Christianity, the state meant the Roman Empire. The Christian Church as a religious community lived in separation and tension with the pagan state. Then in A.D. 312 this separation was changed by the conversion of the Roman emperor Constantine. A new era began in which the Christian religion became the established religion of the Roman state. Yet still there remained, especially in Western Christian thought (as developed by St. Augustine), a sense in which the Church represented a separate religious principle and destiny from that of the secular principle of the state.

This dispute was fanned into new flames with the Reformation. The Anabaptists particularly rejected all alliance between Church and state. The Church was a radically new community of regenerate humanity which must have nothing to do with the instruments of pride, war, and power that characterized the state. Calvinism, as we have seen, took a different approach to this question. The old Catholic or Anglican church-state relations indeed must be repudiated. But there might arise a new reformed state which put itself under the godly ministry of the reformed religion. In this reformed Christian state, the Word of God again became the foundation and constitution for the law of the land. Thus the reformed concept renews the Jewish concepts of a theocratic state governed by the Bible as both moral and legal code. Here the Christian state and its magistracy are included into and bound by the covenant with God. Despite the American separation of Church and state, much of this Calvinist heritage still remains in our characterization of ourselves as a "nation under God."

Some Jews in U.S. have often taken a strict separationist position rather than a theocratic one, thus reversing their position. Some Christians have taken a "Christian Commonwealth" position, thus reversing the early Christian and Anabaptist views.

Another area of dispute has to do with the universality and particularity of the covenant peoplehood. Early Christianity rejected ethnic Israel and with it the connection between the covenant and a particular nation. All nations might belong to the Church. The Church in its mission to the world represented the messianic ingathering of all nations to the one God. Christians, as a people scattered through all races and nations, belong to one people. They are an international people who know no ethnic boundaries.

However, here too we have seen how, in our English and American traditions, there was a reidentification of the New Israel with a particular elect nation. A particular nationality, a particular land, was seen as God's favored instrument of witness in the world. The covenant served also to judge the failings of this particular people, the Anglo-Saxon or American Israel, and to call them into a continual struggle for justice and truth. This new ethnicity of the Christian Israel caused many problems of exclusivity in American history. At first there was a reluctance to admit that other non-Anglo-Saxon, non-Protestant people could belong to the American covenant in the same way as the original stock. Only gradually has the concept of the American covenant lost its White-Anglo-Saxon-Protestant identity in order to accomodate all the various peoples–Black, Brown, Yellow, Red, and White; Catholic, Protestant, and Jewish–who have come to constitute this one nation which has indeed been forged out of many nations.

Today the concept of the New Israel, as a way of reflecting not only on one's religious identity but also on one's ethnic identity, has become important among other new nationalisms. Black Americans, in their search for an authentic identity as displaced Africans, have sometimes found the concept of the New Israel important. Black nationalism is seen as a new instance of a converted people who must stand apart from white society and seek its own identity. Black nationalist Christianity appropriates the theme of Blacks as an elect people, a Black Israel.[20]

The concept of Israel is also important in emerging Asian theology. Kosuke Koyama, the Japanese theologian who has worked in Thailand, speaks of controversy in the Asian Christian soul between two identities: that of Buddha and that of Israel. These symbols express religious dimensions of the struggle between Asian and Western modes of thought and life. The Asian soul must be reformed and renewed by the concept of historical existence that is rooted in the covenant with Israel. Thailand, too, must discover itself as a new Israel.[21]

How did there get to be so many Israels running around among different peoples? How to sort out the relations between them? This clearly is the work of the Christian universal mission to many nations. Missionary work has planted in the hearts of many peoples a model of covenantal existence derived from the Scriptures. Today we might ask ourselves whether it is necessary to think of there being only one "true" Israel, only one elect people. Historically, many peoples, both as religious communities and as political communities, have taken on this covenantal identity. They have accepted the biblical dialectic of judgment and promise as their mode of historical existence.

The covenant is one of the great illuminating paradigms of existence that comes from scriptural revelation. It illuminates life with God and each other. It is valid for whoever adopts it and seeks to live truthfully out of its mandate.

Authentic covenantal life must bring each people to a recognition of its special relation to God. This, in turn, will lead to a struggle to reform and develop justice and reconciliation in their society in fulfillment of God's commands. Perhaps it is time for these many Israels which have been planted throughout the world to see each other not as rivals, but as sister peoples under one God. God is the God of many peoples, each of whom must seek its authentic national destiny in justice and peace within and between nations. In the words of a prophet of the Isaiah tradition: "Blessed be Egypt my people, and Assyria the work of my hands, and Israel my heritage" (Isaiah 19:25).

NOTES

[1]"The Ordinance of God" in *The Library of Christian Classics,* vol. 25, *Spiritual and Anabaptist Writers,* ed. G. H. Williams. (Philadelphia: Westminster Press, 1957), p. 188.

[2]Peter Y. de Jong, *The Covenant Idea in New England Theology: 1620-1847.* (Grand Rapids, Michigan: Eerdmans Publishing Company, 1945), p. 84.

[3]For a history of American Utopianism, see Mark Holloway, *Heavens on Earth: Utopian Communities in America 1680-1880.* (New York: Dover, 1966).

[4]Conrad Cherry, *God's New Israel: Religious Interpretations of America's Destiny.* (Englewood Cliffs, N.J.: Prentice-Hall, 1971), pp. 42-43.

[5]For an explanation of Reformed covenant theology, see Perry Miller, *The New England Mind.* (Cambridge: Harvard University Press, 1939), pp. 365-462.

[6]Michael Wigglesworth, "God's Controversy with New England," in Conrad Cherry, *God's New Israel,* pp. 44-54.

[7]Grindal Rawson, 1709 in Perry Miller, *New England Mind,* pp. 483-4.

[8]Miriam Schneir, ed., *Feminism: The Essential Historical Writings.* (New York: Random House, 1972), pp. 2-3.

[9]*Ibid.*, p. 4.

[10]In Thomas F. Gossett, *Race: The History of an Idea in America.* (New York: Schocken, 1965), pp. 254ff.

[11]*Ibid.,* p. 243.

[12]Stuart Creighton Miller, *The Unwelcome Immigrant: The American Image of the Chinese.* (Berkeley: University of California Press, 1969), p. 170.

[13]Gossett, *Race,* p. 307.

[14]Staughton Lynd, "The Abolitionist Critique of the United States Constitution," in Martin Duberman, ed., *The Anti-Slavery Vanguard: New Essays on the Abolitionists.* (Princeton, N.J.: Princeton University Press, 1965), pp. 209-239.

[15]In Schneir, *Feminism,* pp. 77-80.

[16]C. H. Hopkins, *The Rise of the Social Gospel in American Protestantism, 1865-1915.* (New Haven: Yale University Press, 1940), p. 291.

[17]The phrase comes from Karl Marx, "Economic and Philosophical Manuscripts" in Erich Fromm, *Marx's Concept of Man* (New York: F. Unger, 1961), p. 127.

[18]Paul M. van Buren, *The Burden of Freedom: Americans and the God of Israel.* (New York: Seabury, 1976), p. 81.

[19]Emmanuel Kant, *Religion Within the Limits of Reason Alone.* (New York: Harper and Row, 1960), pp. 113-4.

[20]For example, Albert Cleage, *Black Christian Nationalism.* (New York: Wm. Morrow, 1972).

[21]Gerald H. Anderson, *Asian Voices in Christian Theology.* (Maryknoll, N.Y.: Orbis Books, 1976), pp. 65 ff.

USE GUIDE

Elizabeth L. McWhorter

Introduction

This guide is designed to help individuals and groups explore the basic themes and issues in the twelve chapters of *The Liberating Bond: Covenants–Biblical and Contemporary*. Learning models are suggested for seven general topics through which some of the challenging ideas of the book may be considered and acted upon.

These models are based on an approach to learning known as AAAR: awareness, analysis, action, reflection. True learning–that is, learning which touches our attitudes, actions, and deep feelings–involves these four elements. They do not occur in any regular sequence; often they overlap and intertwine in the learning experience. But they are all there in some combination.

These models suggest procedures through which participants (partners in learning) may broaden and deepen their learning experience.

The guide assumes that participants will be members of a group, large or small. The procedures often call first for individual work which is then related to further activity with a partner or several others. Most of the procedures can best be done in small groups. (Large groups can always be re-formed into several small groups of 5-7 persons each.) Discussion, summary followup action, and evaluation are usually suggested for small working groups, and occasionally for the total group.

Model A, "Living as Partners in Covenant Relationship," is basic and may be used as a self-contained unit. It is essential for Models B-F and should be used prior to any of them. Any one or all of Models B-F may follow Model A in any sequence or combination desired. Model G is self-contained and may be used effectively alone, or in combination with Model A and Models B-F. This flexibility offers a variety of options for those who will plan for the use of *The Liberating Bond*. By selecting, combining, and expanding models to fit particular needs and interests, leaders may plan for a course (13-26 sessions), a short-term study/action series (6-8 sessions), a retreat, seminars.

In the covenant relationship we are challenged to work together on "the inner tensions and the outer edges" of the covenant. The seven models explore four areas of tension or conflict which emerge from covenantal thinking: whether the covenant is primarily external or internal; inclusive or exclusive; eternal or must be renewed; particular (one nation) or universal.

Through creative use of this guide, learners can be helped to see how "our covenant story closes the circle" and to know ourselves "once again addressed as the people of the covenant and invited into a bond that sets us free for each other."

The guide contains frequent references to this resource, *The Liberating Bond: Covenants–Biblical and Contemporary* by Roth and Ruether. There are also some cross references to the companion resource, *Promises to Keep: A Workbook of Experiences for Covenant Living,* by Benson and Benson.

A. Living as Partners in Covenant Relationship

Purpose: To examine our partnerships in relation to God's Covenant relationship.

These exercises may be grouped for one or more sessions as follows: 1-4; 5-7; 8.

1. a. As individuals, make a list of all the relationships *you* are involved in.

b. Make another list of the various *kinds* of relationships that exist in our world today.

2. Find a partner as you begin on these suggestions:

a. Which of the relationships you listed in 1. above would you consider partnerships? Star these on your list.

b. What makes a relationship a partnership?

1) What is the goal of a partnership?

2) What is the role of each partner? What does each partner bring to the relationship?

3) How does the partnership influence the action of each partner? What risks does the partnership present to each person?

4) What are distinctive features of a partnership?

5) Why do we fear partnerships?

3. a. What images, figures of speech, pictures, models would you use to describe a partnership?

b. Summarize your answers to all of questions 2 and 3, using key words and phrases. Put your responses on newsprint to share with the whole group.

c. ". . . a covenant relates the partners as whole persons (or communities) to each other and makes them (fictitious) sisters or brothers of each other. It is a flexible relationship where trust and faithfulness to each other determine the action of the partners." Roth and Ruether, *The Liberating Bond: Covenants–Biblical and Contemporary,* p. 2.

"Covenant-participants (are) . . . persons taken seriously as human beings, living as partners with each other." Roth and Ruether, p. 3.

Consider these quotes as a possible summary of your thinking. Do they reflect your key ideas? What would you add or change?

4. In pairs, consider God's covenant relationship with human beings, using the questions in #2 above and these pages in Roth and Ruether: 5-7; 12-15; 16-17; 30. Compare your responses with those you made to #2. Where are the responses similar? Where different? Discuss with your partner why you think the responses are similar or different. How does the covenant relationship influence the growth of each person in relation to God? Self? Others? The environment?

5. What are the distinctive features in the biblical understanding of God's covenant relationship with Israel?

a. Use Deuteronomy 7:6-11 as basis for answering this question. (See Roth and Ruether, pp. 6-7 for interpretation and summary of this passage.)

b. Do you consider this divine-human relationship a partnership? Why? Prepare a brief summary of your understanding of biblical meaning of *covenant.* (Use pictures, words, and other symbols to convey your ideas. Share.)

6. Roth and Ruether discuss four areas of tension or conflict brought forth by the prevalence of covenantal thinking in ancient Israel. (See pp. 7-8.) Where do you see evidence of these areas of tension in our relationships today?

7. Choose one partnership from your list in #1.

a. Examine this partnership in the light of your understanding of God's covenant relationship with us, using these questions as a guide:

1) In what ways do you feel this partnership is influenced by God's covenant?

2) What do you perceive to be areas of conflict or tension in relation to God's covenant?

3) What changes in the understanding/attitudes/actions of each partner are called for by God's covenant relationship?

b. Identify one element of covenant relationship (see #5 above) you would like to work on in one of your partnerships. Make a list for yourself of what you want to do. Plan to check this list a week later and at regular intervals for the next several weeks.

8. Plan/conduct a service of worship as an experience in which the group celebrates the meaning of community as partnership with God and with each other. (Use ideas from #3 and #5 above.)

You might begin by asking members of the group to form pairs who make a "covenant" vow to each other. (The vow could be part of a creed, or some vow the group draws up together.) Then ask each pair to join with another pair to make this same vow with each other, forming groups of four; repeat this procedure until all groups are re-formed as a total community.

Someone could read Deuteronomy 7:6-11 to identify ourselves as God's covenant people.

Close by asking each member of the original pair to write a prayer/wish of *Shalom* for the other partner. Then use these as offerings.

See Benson and Benson, *Promises to Keep: A Workbook of Experiences for Covenant Living* for other suggestions about ways of working on our relationships in light of God's covenant relationship.

B. Covenant Relationship and Government

Purpose: To evaluate governments (local, state, national, international) in the light of God's covenant relationship.

1. Gather data.

a. Describe your community. What kind of people are in it? Include age, education, economic factors, religious interests, ethnic backgrounds.

b. Now find out everything you can about your local (city/county) government. How is it made up? How are representatives chosen? Who votes? When are elections held? Is the governing body truly representative of the community? Who are elected and who are appointed officials? To whom are they responsible?

c. Interview a member of the City Council or County Governing Board. (Several members of the group may wish to do this and report on their interview to the whole group; or you may wish to invite a Board or Council member to meet with the group and be interviewed by two or three persons. See Benson and Benson, *Promises to Keep,* for helpful techniques in interviewing.) Ask these Council/Board members to review with you the actions of the Council/Board during the past year. What have they accomplished? What are they still working on? How are they trying to meet the needs of the community?

d. After the interview, discuss with the group: What would you like to see added to the Council's/Board's accomplishments? Why? What problems do you feel the Council/Board has? How is the Council/Board trying to solve these problems?

2. Reflect and analyze.

a. Review your understanding of God's covenant relationship (see Model A, #5). Look closely at the four distinctive features of covenant as summarized by Roth and Ruether (pp. 6-7). List the four features separately with space for two responses: (Example)

Mutuality:	*Evidence for*	*Evidence against*

b. Evaluate your local government (city/county) using these four features as criteria. How did you rate your government? Why? Compare your analysis with that of others in the group.

3. Act. (Work on one or more of these suggestions; add your own.)

a. Using the results of your analysis in #2 above, make a list (individually, in pairs, as a group) of improvements or changes needed in governments in light of God's covenant relationship. Arrange items on this list in order of priority and select one of your top three suggestions to work on (e.g., better-qualified Council/Board members).

Describe appropriate action(s) you as an individual or your group could take. (Get more information on background of present Council/Board members; interview more people in the community about qualifications needed; interview Council/Board members about their position on key issues.) Sharpen up your thinking; then decide on next steps you and others in your group will take.

You might decide to run as a candidate in the next election and work on your own platform! (Get reactions from the group as you build your platform.)

b. Select one area of interest or concern to you (e.g., Foreign Policy, World Hunger, Economic and Social Justice, Ecology, Human Rights, Welfare, Education). Go through the same procedure you used in #3a as you work on other governments or government agencies—state, national, international. (Use Roth and Ruether, pp. 68-72, 76-80, and Benson and Benson, as resources for this exercise.)

c. In light of your understanding of God's covenant relationship, how do you react to these paragraphs written in October 1976 by church leaders in Latin American countries in this *Open Letter to North American Christians*?

> Friends and fellow Christians, it is time that you realize that our continent is becoming one gigantic prison, and in some regions one vast cemetery; that human rights, the grand guidelines of the Gospel, are becoming a dead letter, without force. And all this in order to maintain a system, a structure of dependency, that benefits the mighty privileged persons of your land and of our land at the expense of the poor millions who are increasing throughout the width and breadth of the continent.
>
> For this reason this open letter seeks to be the lamentation or the outcry of those who now have no voice in our America, because they are buried in the volcanoes, the rivers or the cemeteries; because they are rotting in prisons or concentration camps; or because they languish in incredible conditions of malnutrition and misery. This letter seeks to be an anguished, fervent call to your conscience and to your responsibility as Christians.

> If in the past you felt it to be your apostolic duty to send us missionaries and economic resources, today the frontier of your witness and Christian solidarity is within your own country. The conscious, intelligent and responsible use of your vote, the appeal to your representatives in the Congress, and the application of pressure by various means on your authorities can contribute to changing the course of our governments toward paths of greater justice and brotherhood or to accentuating a colonist and oppressive policy over our peoples. In this sense you must ask yourselves if you will or will not be "your brother's keeper" in these lands of America, from which the blood of millions of Abels is clamoring to heaven.
>
> We, between tears and groans, are interceding for you in order that you may respond with faithfulness to the historic responsibility that as citizens of one of the great contemporary powers and as disciples of Jesus Christ it falls on you to assume.

In small groups, compose a pastoral letter as a response to these Latin American church leaders.

d. Have a debate on the topic, "Resolved: that the idea of God's covenant relationship has influenced theories of government in Western civilization." (See Roth and Ruether, pp. 48; 60-65; 67-89, for development of this idea.) In small groups, work on a positive or negative response to this issue. Hold the debate with two persons giving a positive response and two persons making a negative response. Allow time for brief rebuttals from each side. Then have the group vote on which presentation (positive or negative) wins the debate.

Now discuss why you agree/disagree with Roth and Ruether's thesis. What evidence of the influence of covenant relationship do you see in theories of government in other parts of the world, such as Eastern civilizations? The Third World? (See Roth and Ruether, p. 90-91.)

e. Role-play a meeting of a governing group, such as a state/nation legislative body, an administrative council, an international court of justice. Choose a current issue for consideration, such as peace in the Middle East, Panama Canal Treaty, criminal justice, shipment of grain to underdeveloped countries, human rights. As a group, sharpen up an agenda item for consideration at this meeting. Then ask for 5-7 volunteers to do a role-play as members of the governing group to consider this issue. Allow 10-12 minutes for the role play. (Do not necessarily expect the group to solve the issue, or even to come to any clear conclusion.)

After the role-play, a person designated beforehand should lead a discussion. Reflect first with role-players only, using these questions:

1) How did you feel about what was going on?
2) Why did the governing body act/fail to act on the issue?
3) What steps should the governing body take in the future?
4) What are your learnings from this experience?

Now reflect with the whole group:

1) What learnings from this role-play apply to your participation in government at each level–local, state, national, international?

2) What kind of resources and support should government representatives have?

3) What new/different understanding of government do you now have?

4) What is our responsibility in government in relation to God's covenant relationship? (Use Roth and Ruether, pp. 10-25 as you work on this question.)

f. Brainstorm a list of ways that government actions/legislation can reflect God's covenant relationship. During the next week check the news (TV, newspapers, magazines) for actions which you feel affirm/deny God's covenant relationship. Share these with the group at the next meeting. Discuss possible follow-up action.

See Benson and Benson for additional information, ideas, and suggestions for exploring the area of government and God's covenant relationship.

C. Minorities in Covenant Relationship

Purpose: To explore in a group (which includes persons of various ethnic groups in your community) ways in which "Shalom" can become more of a reality for these groups.

1. a. In small groups (3-5), summarize the participation of ethnic groups in American life from the beginning of America to the present day. (For example, consider the role of Blacks, American Indians, Latin Americans. See Roth and Ruether, pp. 69-82.)

b. What problems now keep each of these groups from full participation in the mainstream of American political life? (Consider economics, education, social and religious factors and relate to your own community in terms of voting practices, schools, employment, housing, churches.)

For example, in January 1978, unemployment for the nation as a whole was 6.8%, but 40% for young Blacks. What are the figures for your community? Make specific suggestions about what can be done locally to help this problem. What can be done nationally? What steps will you take now?

2. a. Interview one or more members of ethnic groups in your community. (See Benson and Benson for helpful interview techniques.) Ask them to share their experience of living as members of American democratic society.

Give a brief talk (5 minutes) on the meaning of the covenant relationship in American democracy as presented by Roth and Ruether (see pp. 48-65). Ask persons of ethnic groups to respond to these ideas.

b. Dialogue in pairs about the meaning of the covenant themes of "privileges" and "judgment" (responsibility)—see Roth and Ruether, pp. 10, 23, and 65-66 in relation to problems of minority persons/groups. What changes in your community will have to occur in order for persons of ethnic groups to be fully participating members of our nation? Decide on criteria you will use to identify these changes. Then make a list of suggestions in order of priority.

c. Select one of your first three priorities. Think of several specific actions which would help to bring about change in this area. Which of these actions could take place in your community?

d. Choose one of these actions you can begin to work on now. Discuss it with others (a partner or the whole group). Agree on specific steps you will follow in the next several weeks/months. Set definite times for check-ins, using these questions as guides for evaluation:

- What have you accomplished to date?
- What still needs to be done?
- What are the next steps?
- Who needs to do what?
- How effective do you feel this course of action to be?
- What are your learnings?

3. Reflect on goals of the covenant relationship. (See Roth and Ruether, pp. 6-8; 17.)

In what ways do persons of ethnic groups in your community seem to be moving toward wholeness (shalom)? In what ways do the lives of these persons seem broken, shattered?

Dialogue about what helps/hinders the realization of wholeness in your community. Explore possible next steps your group can take to work for more wholeness for all persons in your community. Plan to take appropriate action; schedule some times for check-up and evaluation.

D. International Relations and God's Covenant Relationship

Purpose: To consider current international concerns in the light of covenant relationships.

1. a. Become familiar with the Old Testament Book of Jonah (4 chapters in length). Read it several times. Then summarize the action of this short drama in outline form; list the main characters and the key ideas. What is the main theme of the book? (See Roth and Ruether, pp. 25-27.)

b. Now try your hand at writing the scenario for a twentieth-century version of Jonah. Ask members of your group to provide words and action to go along with your scenario. Then talk together about these questions: What is the underlying theme of your drama? How have you developed the theme? What is the outcome of the drama? How is it similar/different from the outcome of Jonah?

2. a. Jonah's experience taught him that God's love is universal and not centered on just one favored nation. He learned, reluctantly, that he had responsibility for bringing God's judgment and mercy to other nations. In light of Jonah's experience, consider our role as North Americans in relation to other nations of the world. What attitudes/actions are called for on our part because of our "covenants" in our dealings with other nations? As you work on this question, consider these areas:

Mainland China (See *China: Search for Community,* Whitehead)
South Korea
Mexican immigrants
Palestine
Israel
Egypt
Panama
Cuba
India
South Africa

Look at our relationships in these areas with regard to such concerns as boundaries (limit, extend); export-import; immigration; quotas; aid to underdeveloped countries; arms limitation; local self-rule; social and economic justice.

b. Focus on one particular concern in one particular nation. (Reflect on Roth and Ruether, pp. 9-11, as you work on this section. See also Isaiah 2:2-4; 49:6; Micah 4:1-4.) Check to see if there is some legislation pending in Congress that relates to this concern. State why you would support the legislation or how you would change it so that you could support it. If no legislation is pending, draft a proposed recommendation for consideration by Congress. Give reasons to support your recommendation.

c. Examine the denial of human rights in South Africa in relation to the goal of God's covenant relationship. Look for news reports in the media of what is currently happening in that country where the population is composed of 20 million blacks, and 4 million whites. On October 19, 1977, "The South African Government embarked . . . on a massive crackdown on dissent against its racial policies, banning 18 civil rights groups, shutting down two major black newspapers and arresting scores of black and white anti-apartheid leaders," according to a report in the *Washington Post.* The *New York Times* stated:

"The groups that were proscribed included the affiliates of the Black Consciousness movement, whose leader, Steven Biko, died in custody last month of causes still not determined. Also banned were the Christian Institute of Southern Africa, an ecumenical group that has been a critic of racial policies, and its leader, the Rev. Beyers Naude."

What would the covenant goal of wholeness (shalom) mean for blacks in South Africa? For whites? (Reflect on Roth and Ruether, pp. 12-14, as you think about this question.)

What is the position of the United States government in relation to South Africa? What influence might the government position have in helping to secure human rights for all persons in South Africa? Is this a position you can support? Why?

Consider sending a letter to the South African ambassador to this country (U.S. Ambassador Donald B. Sole, Embassy of South Africa, 3051 Massachusetts Ave., N.W., Washington, DC 20008) setting forth your views in relation to the crisis of human rights in South Africa. You may also want to send copies of your letter to the President of the United States, your senators, and your representatives.

E. Jewish/Christian Relations and Covenant Relationship

Purpose: To explore, in a group made up of persons from the Jewish and Christian communities, the meaning of God's covenant relationship as a basis for better understanding of one another.

Make arrangements for an exploratory meeting of persons from Jewish and Christian communities (10-20 persons, preferably half from each community). Plan for an initial meeting to identify some of your assumptions in relation to each other; then consider plans for a series of follow-up discussions. These suggestions can guide you in this procedure:

1. The initial meeting.

a. Spend some time getting acquainted with one another. Ask each person to tell about her/his family relationship, work, one special hobby or interest.

b. What are similarities/differences in Jewish/Christian understanding of covenant? Each person first writes answers to this question—then dialogue in pairs (one from each community) about responses.

c. In groups of four, look at Roth and Ruether's interpretation of Jewish/Christian interpretation of covenant. (See pp. 2-3, 28-29, 32-42, 84-87.) Agree/disagree?

d. How would Christians/Jews react to these issues? (In pairs, discuss answers for a given length of time. Then ask each pair to summarize their responses to each issue in a word or phrase. Write the responses on newsprint or chalkboard for the whole group.)

- U.S. foreign policy in the Middle East
- Arab nations
- Religious holidays
- Government welfare programs

(Save these responses to use again later—see #3a below.)

e. As a group, brainstorm a list of topics for productive discussion (write these down). Then ask pairs to choose three most important topics and select one to begin with. Share with the total group and, if possible, get quick consensus on three topics to pursue in future meetings of the group. If there is wide divergence, a small committee (equal number from each community) may be asked to make the final selection and plan for future meetings.

f. Ask each person to write out answers to this question: What are my expectations from these discussions? Give responses to the Steering Committee to use in their planning.

2. Decide on x number of meetings for a study/discussion based on response to the first session. As a group, formulate a statement of purpose for these meetings. At the close of the series, plan for a worship service to celebrate new learnings and new relationships which have begun.

3. a. At the last session of the series, ask each person to answer again the questions in #1d above and compare with answers given in the first session. Are there any changes in your responses? Why? If possible, dialogue with original partners from the first session, or with another partner about these responses.

b. Evaluate this series:

1) What new/different understandings/attitudes do you have as a result of your experiences in this series?

2) What has been helpful to you? What has been difficult?

3) What follow-up steps to continue the Jewish/Christian dialogue do you plan to take as a result of this experience?

Another excellent suggestion for exploration of the meaning of covenant may be found in Benson and Benson, *Promises to Keep.* Six basic factors in the making of covenants are examined in relation to Joshua 24.

F. The Church and God's Covenant Relationship

Purpose: To examine the life of your congregation in light of God's covenant relationship.

1. a. List a variety of organizations in your community, such as: labor union, Rotary, glee club, football team, drama group, book club, Junior League, Little League, etc. Make a list of the similarities/differences between these organizations and your church. Be sure to include these categories:

- requirements for becoming a member
- privileges of membership
- duties of membership
- relation of members to each other
- symbolic expressions of membership
- rituals of membership
- outcomes (rewards) of membership

b. Reflect on biblical covenants, using these questions as guides:

Who are the partners in the covenant?
How is the covenant entered into?
What responsibility does the covenant place on the partners?
What symbols and rituals are used to express the covenant relationship?
What are the outcomes of covenant relationship?
How does the covenant partnership affect the building of community?

Work on one or more of these scripture passages as you deal with the above questions:

Joshua 24
Deuteronomy 7:6-11;29:10-15;30:15
2 Kings 23:1-3
Isaiah 42:6; 54:9-10.
1 Corinthians 11:23-26,31-34
2 Corinthians 3:6-8,17-19
Hebrews 9:15

2. a. In small groups (5 persons or less) consider the meaning of church membership as expressed in your congregation. Use the questions in #1 above to focus your thinking. As you reflect on your own experience in this congregation, discuss those features which help to build community and those which hinder.

How and when are new members received in your congregation? What preparation is there? What follow-up?

b. Plan a procedure for receiving new members into your congregation which might express more effectively your understanding of "covenant relationship" than the procedure now being used. Present your plan to your pastor and governing board for consideration. Be available to help carry out and evaluate your plan.

3. In what ways does the worship of your congregation reflect the meaning of covenant partnership?

a. Evaluate a service of worship:

1) When do you feel most involved? Least involved?

2) What symbols (visual, verbal) help remind you of covenant as a "liberating bond"?

3) In what ways does the worship enable *all* members of your congregation to participate fully? (Children, youth, adults; men, women; ethnic groups; married couples, singles; employed, unemployed.)

4) How does the service help members to enter into the community and worldwide dimensions of the covenant?

b. Plan/conduct a service of worship which you feel can enable all members of the congregation to experience the covenant as "shalom" (wholeness) in their own lives. (See Roth and Ruether, pp. 14, 16-17.)

4. a. Think about the last time you participated in an observance of the Lord's Supper. What were your main impressions? (Respond by writing words or short phrases, or by drawing pictures.) Share these with a partner. Then discuss: What meanings should the Lord's Supper convey? (Roth and Ruether, pp. 41-42 provides a stimulating discussion of this question. Use 1 Cor. 11:23-26, 33-34; 2 Cor. 3:6-8, 17-19; and Hebrews 9:15 in thinking through your response.)

b. In pairs, plan for a service of worship which includes the Lord's Supper and which reflects our covenant relationship. Consider all aspects of the service as you plan—the setting, the arrangement of the room, ways in which those present will participate, what will be included in the service. When you have completed plans for the service, ask these questions:

1) What features of this service will help participants feel that they are partners in this covenant relationship with each other and with God?

2) In what ways will this service remind participants of their responsibility to extend this covenant relationship into every area of life?

3) How will this service convey the meaning of the Lord's Supper? (See #4a above.)

5. a. Roth and Ruether discuss the role of "intentional communities" in relation to the church (see pp. 45-52). Many such communities have been and are a part of the life of this country. In addition to the ones mentioned in the book, you may know of others, such as the Koinonia Community near Americus, Georgia. If you live near one of these communities, you may want to make plans to visit (check ahead with members of the community), or invite one or two members of the community to visit your group for an interview session. Try to find out what is the special "intention" of the community. What is the motivation for joining the community? What are the strengths/weaknesses of the community? (See Benson and Benson for suggestions about interviewing.)

After the visit or the interview, reflect as a group on how the community seems to express, or fail to express, covenant relationship. Then discuss how your church seems to express, or fail to express, covenant relationship. What is the role of such intentional communities in relation to the church? What particular needs does this community seem to meet?

6. Consider the world-wide implications of covenant relationship. (Roth and Ruether offer biblical and historical resources for this topic. See pp. 9-12, 22-24, 25-27, 89-91.) Before the next meeting of your group, collect news items (reports/pictures/editorials) about various parts of the world to make a collage. After sharing these items with the whole group, choose one particular area and write a "pastoral" letter to Christians in the church there. Each person should write a letter and then share it with the group in some way (read aloud or display on wall). Explore the possibility of mailing some of these letters. (Check with your denomination's International Mission agency.)

7. Reflect on the following statement by Billy Graham in light of God's covenant relationship.

> In an interview published in the January 1978 issue of *McCall's* magazine, Evangelist Billy Graham says he "used to play God, but I can't do that anymore. . . . I used to believe that pagans in far-off countries were lost–were going to hell–if they did not have the Gospel of Jesus Christ preached to them." Graham says, "I no longer believe that. I believe that there are other ways of recognizing the existence of God–through nature, for instance–and plenty of other opportunities, therefore, of saying 'yes' to God."
>
> He was asked about people like Jews who do not accept Christ as Savior. His answer was: "God does the saving. I'm told to preach Christ as the only way to salvation. But it is God who is going to do the judging, not Billy Graham."
>
> He also said he is more tolerant with other kinds of Christians. "My contact with Catholic, Lutheran and other leaders–people far removed from my own Southern Baptist tradition–has helped me, hopefully, to move in the right direction."

Do you agree/disagree with his position? Why?

What are the implications of his statement for the church's mission?

How does his statement reflect God's covenant relationship? Discuss your responses in small groups.

(For additional suggestions about ways to explore The Church and Covenant Relationship, see Benson and Benson, *Promises to Keep,* II A, B. C.)

G. The Future and Covenant Relationship

Purpose: To express the implications of covenant relationship in several areas of human experience.

"Wave a magic wand" and imagine what would be happening at some future date if there were true covenant partnership in various relationships. What would it look like if "persons were taking each other seriously as human beings"? (Use any one of these areas, several of them, or all of them as interest and time permit.)

1. As you begin this exercise, reflect on covenant as it relates to past, present, and future. (See Roth and Ruether, pp. 31-34, 65-66, 87-88, 89-91. Reflect on Jer. 31:31-34; Ezek. 36:22-28;37:1-14 to see how these Old Testament writers dreamed of the future.)

Identify the "roots" of covenant on which you will build your fantasy. See Roth and Ruether, pp. 6-7, for the basic elements of covenant relationship. Write out your own descriptions of these elements.

2. Dream about the *relation of men and women in society.* In small groups, make a list of major problems in this area.

(Roth and Ruether, pp. 53-57, looks at problems of the marriage relationship in light of the imagery used in Ephesians 5:21-30. What are the implications of Ruether's interpretation of this passage for the marriage relationship? For all the relations of men and women? How do you react to this interpretation in light of God's covenant relationship?)

Be sure that your list deals with problems of both single and married persons, and divorced, widowed, and homosexual persons. Use the list of basic elements of covenant you developed in #1 above to describe in some way (draw, dramatize, write description) how you envision men/women relations in the future. Include such areas of experience as family, business, education, political life, religion, social life, cultural life, marriage, employment. (See Roth and Ruether, pp. 68-69, and Benson and Benson, for helpful ideas and suggestions related to this issue.)

3. How would you envision *prison reform?*

a. Consider these factors:

> About 75% of all arrests nationwide are of persons 23 years or younger.
>
> From 95-98% of prison inmates will return to the community at some time.
>
> Prison administrators estimate that 65-90% of prisoners do not need to be incarcerated to protect society.
>
> It costs from $6,000-$25,000 per year to incarcerate someone, depending on the state, the cost of imprisonment, the loss of taxes on wages, and costs of families that must go on welfare or be placed in foster homes.
>
> It costs about $400-$600 per year to supervise someone on probation or to place him/her in a work-release program in which inmates pay for their room and board.
>
> "The wheels of criminal justice should turn in the effort to *restore the wholeness of the community.* In many so-called primitive societies, especially in Africa, that is the goal in practice. A case is not completed in many an African village or tribal council, until victim and family are reconciled with offender and family in such a way as to draw the whole disrupted community together. Often it is far from being easy. It would be even harder here in our complex society, but only as we work for that goal can we hope to heal the wounds that are both causes and effects of crime."—L. Harold DeWolf.

b. Reflect on this issue in light of discussion in Roth and Ruether, pp. 9-12, 76-81, 87-88, following the same procedure suggested in #1 and #2 above:

1) Identify the root elements of covenant.

2) List problems related to the area of prison reform.

3) Envision a future (or next steps) for prison reform which in some way reflects covenant relationship.

As you work on this project, consider the whole system of criminal justice. Become familiar with the problems and needs in your own community as well as in the nation and those in countries like Mexico, Chile, South Africa, Korea.

4. How would you picture *church-state relations*?

Roth and Ruether, in pp. 46-47, 60-61, 88-89, trace the varied patterns of church-state relations from the time of ancient Israel up to the present time. Make a brief outline of this historical development. List the advantages/disadvantages of (1) separation of church and state and (2) union of church and state.

In small groups, discuss problems that arise from these two patterns. Review again the root elements of covenant (see #1 above). Now describe in some way (write brief description, dramatize, draw) how you envision a future in which church/state relations truly express covenant partnership. Share with other groups and discuss. Evaluate the future you have imagined in terms of the basic covenant elements; make needed revisions.

5. Consider your congregation as a covenant partnership. How would you state the overall mission goal of your congregation? (Look again carefully at these sections in Roth and Ruether: pp. 9-10, 12-15, 18, 59, 89-91.) Examine its life and work in light of root covenant elements (see #1 above). You may want to invite your minister(s) and some of your governing board to join you for this exploration. Be sure to include such areas as worship, education, service, stewardship, evangelism, outreach, administration, and local, national, and international expressions. Look at all facets of your program: services of worship; church school; your church's ministry with children, with youth, with adults; new membership courses; budget; projects; and community relations.

How do the life and work of your congregation reflect/fail to reflect covenant relationship?

Now "wave a magic wand" and imagine a congregation which truly expresses covenant relationship. Who would belong? Where would it be? What would be its underlying purpose? What would its worship be like? What rituals or symbols would it use? What kinds of actions and programs would it undertake? How would it worship? What would be the role of leaders? How would its members relate to one another? To others?

Share your dream with a partner; with another group. Which parts of your dream could you begin to work on now in your own congregation? Decide on a next step and agree on checkup points.

6. Other areas. Resource material for dealing with at least two other areas—world hunger and ecology—may be found in Benson and Benson *Promises to Keep.*

a. For suggestions about world hunger. Dream about a world in which all persons have enough to eat. Evaluate your dream in light of the meaning of the Good Samaritan.

b. For suggestions about ecology. Envision a world in which natural resources are being consumed, enjoyed, and replenished when possible by human beings as stewards of God's creation. How would such a world reflect God's covenant relationship?